Multilingual Teaching

Full details of all our publications can be found on https://www.
multilingual-matters.com, or by writing to Multilingual Matters,
St Nicholas House, 31–34 High Street, Bristol, BS1 2AW, UK.

Multilingual Teaching

The Missing Piece

Roma Chumak-Horbatsch

MULTILINGUAL MATTERS
Bristol • Jackson

DOI https://doi.org/10.21832/CHUMAK0947
Library of Congress Cataloging in Publication Data
A catalog record for this book is available from the Library of Congress.
Names: Chumak-Horbatsch, Roma, author.
Title: Multilingual Teaching: The Missing Piece/Roma Chumak-Horbatsch.
Description: Bristol; Jackson: Multilingual Matters, [2025] | Includes
  bibliographical references. | Summary: "This book lays out a radical new
  approach for teaching in multilingual classrooms: to include everyone,
  including those who already speak the school language, in multilingual
  pedagogy. The author proposes Linguistically Appropriate Practice Plus,
  a new resource to help teachers support the language interests of school
  language speakers"— Provided by publisher.
Identifiers: LCCN 2024029645 (print) | LCCN 2024029646 (ebook) | ISBN
  9781800410947 (hardback) | ISBN 9781800410930 (paperback) | ISBN
  9781800410954 (pdf) | ISBN 9781800410961 (epub)
Subjects: LCSH: Multilingual education.
Classification: LCC LC3715 .C493 2025 (print) | LCC LC3715 (ebook) | DDC
  370.117/5—dc23/eng/20240928
LC record available at https://lccn.loc.gov/2024029645
LC ebook record available at https://lccn.loc.gov/2024029646

British Library Cataloguing in Publication Data
A catalogue entry for this book is available from the British Library.

ISBN-13: 978-1-80041-094-7 (hbk)
ISBN-13: 978-1-80041-093-0 (pbk)

Multilingual Matters
UK: St Nicholas House, 31–34 High Street, Bristol, BS1 2AW, UK.
USA: Ingram, Jackson, TN, USA.

Website: https://www.multilingual-matters.com
X: Multi_Ling_Mat
Facebook: https://www.facebook.com/multilingualmatters
Blog: https://www.channelviewpublications.wordpress.com

The policy of Multilingual Matters/Channel View Publications is to use
papers that are natural, renewable and recyclable products, made from wood
grown in sustainable forests. In the manufacturing process of our books, and
to further support our policy, preference is given to printers that have FSC and
PEFC Chain of Custody certification. The FSC and/or PEFC logos will appear
on those books where full certification has been granted to the printer
concerned.

Typeset by Techset Composition India(P) Ltd, Bangalore and Chennai, India.

To Marko

Registered Trademark

LINGUISTICALLY APPROPRIATE
PRACTICE®

Application Number: 1885633

Certification of Registration: June 15, 2021

Registration Number: 1,102,068

Contents

Acknowledgements   ix

Introduction   xi

Multilingual Teaching and Learning Glossary   xxi

The Missing Piece Investigation: Themes and Topics

Theme 1	The Backstory: How it all Happened	3
Theme 2	School Language Speakers: A Language Profile	8
Theme 3	LAP+: A New Resource	15
Theme 4	LAP+ Stands Strong	22
Theme 5	The Language-Rich Classroom	28
Theme 6	LAP+ Teachers	35
Theme 7	LAP+ in Action	43
Theme 8	How Language Works	54

In Closing …   91

Index   96

Acknowledgements

A very warm and special thank you - *merci - grazie - дякую* to the teachers, who, in the challenging COVID period, embraced LAP+, reached out to school language speakers, engaged them in meaningful language tasks and enriched their language lives. By extending multilingual teaching to former school language learners and native school language speakers, these LAP+ pioneers demonstrated that multilingual teaching can indeed go further and do more! A special THANK YOU, also, to Anna Roderick and the entire MM Team for making this book happen.

Introduction

An Unexpected Discovery

As the COVID pandemic closed everything down in early 2020, I started thinking about the next step in my multilingual teaching journey. As I reviewed stacks of field notes and records from my years-long international work in multilingual teaching, conducted a professional self-audit and reread the multilingual teaching guidebooks I authored (Chumak-Horbatsch, 2012, 2019), I made an unexpected discovery. I found that school language speakers were missing from the multilingual teaching agenda. While school language learners took center stage and received extensive language support, attention, encouragement and help, their school language-speaking classmates remained on the sidelines, shut out of multi-language activities. Here are two examples from my field notes:

> Watching a group of classmates prepare bilingual name cards using shiny paper and coloured markers, a seven-year old speaker of English (the school language) timidly approached the teacher, pointed to the name card activity and said: *I can't do that because I have English*

> During preparations for a school-wide multilingual and multicultural celebration, a group of grade six speakers of English (the school language) told their teacher:
> *'We can't help because we speak English. It's not for us.'*

This discovery of exclusion and language support imbalance became a *chiodo fisso* or a fixed idea in my head. It led me to identify school language speakers as the missing piece in multilingual teaching and ask: *Were these learners absent from the multilingual teaching program because they were speakers of the school language?* When a search of language teaching journals, reports and publications provided no information, I reached out (via Zoom) to teachers I had worked with to ask about school language speakers. Here is what they reported:

- the multilingual teaching program is intended for school language *learners*;
- information about the language backgrounds of school language speakers is sparse;
- they have an academic advantage and do not need language support; and
- they often serve as translators to help their school language-learning classmates.

The Missing Piece Investigation

 The sparse information about school language speakers prompted me to take on this unexplored topic. To guide the missing piece investigation, I formulated five questions:

(1) Who are school language speakers? What is their language reality?
(2) Should proficiency in the school language exempt learners from participating in multi-language activities?
(3) Is there a place for school language speakers in the multilingual teaching agenda?
(4) Has the attention to school language learners and the urgency to help, integrate and support them overshadowed the language skills, experiences and interests of school language speakers?
(5) Is current multilingual teaching fully inclusive? Is it linguistically fair?

Goals

My approach to the missing piece investigation was qualitative and inquisitive. As I entered this new research cave (Slekar, 2005), I wanted to unravel and understand the language reality of school language speakers, think about bringing them into the multilingual teaching agenda, share my findings with the multilingual teaching community and initiate a dialogue about these overlooked learners. With this in mind, I set three goals to provide direction to the investigation:

• characterize the language circumstance of school language speakers;
• make a case for bringing them into the multilingual teaching program; and

- prepare a teaching resource that addresses their unique language interests and needs.

Data Source

From my field notes, I selected and analyzed 45 entries that made reference to, or described language behaviors of school language speakers. These included direct observations in various learning contexts (preschools, elementary school classrooms, hallways, lunchrooms and schoolyards and specialized programs) and also interactions with teachers, learners and families.

Five reasons why this matters

(1) The language reality of school language speakers in language-rich classrooms is an overlooked topic in multilingual teaching research.
(2) Excluding learners is wrong and unlawful for two reasons:
   (i) It violates school board equity and inclusion curriculum policies and mission statements that govern public education. Here is an example from the Toronto District School Board, the largest and one of the most diverse school boards in Canada: '... *fairness, equity and inclusion are essential principles ... integrated into all policies, programs, operations and practices*'.[1]
   (ii) It stands in contrast to the two main support pillars of multilingual teaching: language inclusion and language fairness (Chumak-Horbatsch, 2019).
(3) The missing piece investigation responds to the call put forward by García and Flores (2012: 244)

to *experiment, innovate and expand* multilingual pedagogies to better understand *linguistically heterogeneous classrooms and the language* demands of the 21st century.
(4) Bringing school language speakers on board decenters multilingual teaching from its traditional focus on school language learners.
(5) Engagement in the multilingual teaching program extends and enriches the language lives of school language speakers.

Is This Book for You?

If you work in a language-rich classroom, adopt multilingual teaching to support school language learners, then *Multilingual Teaching: The Missing Piece* is for you. It will turn your attention to school language speakers and help you understand their language reality. The new hands-on resource will help you support and enrich the language lives of these overlooked learners and make your multilingual teaching fully inclusive and linguistically fair.

Plan of the Book

Multilingual teaching and learning glossary

This alphabetical list includes words, phrases, key terms, expressions and concepts that are central to the understanding of multilingual teaching and learning. While glossaries are traditionally found in the back matter (or end) of a book, this glossary is placed at the readers' fingertips, in the front matter (or beginning), allowing for quick access to terms used throughout the book.

Missing piece investigation: Themes and topics

The eight themes and 49 topics that make up the missing piece investigation include background information; a language profile of school language speakers; a new resource called LAP + ; a description of language-rich classrooms; a portrayal of teachers who extend multilingual practice to school language speakers and a language information depository. Here is a snapshot of each theme.

Themes

1. The Backstory: How it all Happened
2. School Language Speakers: A Language Profile
3. LAP+: A New Resource
4. LAP+ Stands Strong
5. Language-Rich Classrooms
6. LAP+ Teachers
7. LAP+ in Action
8. How Language Works

Theme 1: The Backstory: How it all Happened

The opening theme sets the stage for the missing piece investigation and positions language support in language-rich classrooms in the wider multilingual teaching picture. The evolution of a widely used multilingual teaching resource called Linguistically Appropriate Practice or LAP (Chumak-Horbatsch, 2012, 2019) is used to make a case for extending multilingual teaching to learners who already speak the school language, to acknowledge their language richness and support their language interests.

Theme 2: School Language Speakers: A Language Profile

This theme describes the language reality of school language speakers and explains why they belong in the multilingual teaching agenda. The language profiles of two very different school language speakers are included.

Theme 3: LAP+: A New Resource

The third theme introduces LAP+ and describes it as a much-needed multilingual teaching resource that engages school language speakers in language tasks.

Theme 4: LAP+ Stands Strong

The fourth theme reassures readers that extending language support to school language speakers is a pedagogical step that has solid support and backing.

Theme 5: Language-Rich Classrooms

Language-rich or multilingual classrooms are described as unique and diverse learning spaces where the language skills and interests of *all* learners are acknowledged, enriched and extended.

Theme 6: LAP+ Teachers

Like learners, LAP+ teachers have rich and varied language backgrounds. Serving as language role models, language guardians and language organizers, they advocate fully inclusive multilingual teaching.

Theme 7: LAP+ in Action

This theme describes how language engagement, the main LAP+ strategy, is adopted with two real school language speakers. This strategy includes language discussions, activity selection, active participation, choice, documenting benefits gained and suggestions for language task assessment.

Theme 8: How Language Works

The final theme provides readers with background information that will extend and strengthen their understanding of language, help them plan a multilingual agenda, respond to language interests, questions and concerns, and promote bi/multilingualism.

Notes and References

Notes and references appear at the end of each theme. Notes are explanations and clarifications of specific topics and issues included in the themes. References are alphabetical lists of cited sources.

They acknowledge authors and provide retrieval information for readers who want to know more.

Reading Features

Multilingual Teaching: The Missing Piece is a small book with a big message. Prepared with the busy teacher in mind, it includes 10 features that have been identified as *important* by teachers and make the book easy and quick to navigate:

- bolded and *italicized* words, citations and terms;
- catchy and appealing titles and subtitles;
- question and answer (Q and A) blue boxes;
- simple and clear visuals;
- bulleted lists;
- short, action-driven sentences;
- brief and easy to read explanations;
- manageable text blocks;
- reader-friendly writing style; and
- references for additional reading.

Reading Suggestions

(1) Think about the school language speakers in your classroom. What do you know about their language backgrounds and interests?
(2) Read *Multilingual Teaching: The Missing Piece* on your own.
(3) Organize a reading club and include *Multilingual Teaching: The Missing Piece* on the reading list.
(4) Discuss and share ideas, teaching strategies and resources with colleagues.

Note

(1) https://www.tdsb.on.ca/Elementary-School/The-Classroom/Equity-Inclusion CH 2012

References

Chumak-Horbatsch, R. (2012) *Linguistically Appropriate Practice: A Guide for Working with Young Immigrant Children*. University of Toronto Press.

Chumak-Horbatsch, R. (2019) *Using Linguistically Appropriate Practice: A Guide for Teaching in Multilingual Classrooms*. Multilingual Matters.

García, O. and Flores, N. (2012) Multilingual pedagogies. In O. García and N. Flores (eds) *The Routledge Handbook of Multilingualism* (pp. 232–246). Routledge

Slekar, T.D. (2005) Without 1, where would we begin? Small sample research in educational settings. *Journal of Thought* 40 (1), 79–86.

Multilingual Teaching and Learning Glossary

What is a Glossary?

A glossary is a mini dictionary or an alphabetical list of words and terms that are important to a specific subject, text or topic. This multilingual teaching glossary is an alphabetical list of words, phrases, key terms, expressions and concepts that are central to the understanding of multilingual teaching.

Age-appropriate means suitable for a specific age or age group. It is used to determine the suitability of topics, materials or activities for learners' level of understanding, interest, and/or developmental readiness.

A *bilingual* is a person with some level of proficiency in two languages. People become bilingual either by acquiring two languages in childhood, or by learning a second language after acquiring their first language. When the productive suffix *-ism* is added to bilingual, we have *bilingualism* which refers to the state or condition of using two languages.

The term *bi/multilingual*, a combination of bilingual and multilingual, is used to refer to a person who speaks two or more languages. In the same way, bi/multilingualism refers to the state or condition of using more than two languages and is used in the book for purposes of brevity and ease of reading.

Diversity means varied or different. Diversity exists in nature, in the many living things that exist on the planet. These include different plants, trees, animals, insects, oceans, forests, mountain environments and coral reefs. Diversity in humans includes visible differences such as age, ethnicity, language, gender, physical qualities and race, while invisible diversity includes educational background and life experiences. The terms *linguistic diversity* or *linguistically diverse*, then, refer to language differences, language variation or the presence of many different languages.

A *dominant language* is the stronger or most often used language of a bi/multilingual.

A *home or family language* is a language or a version of a language, such as a dialect, that is most commonly used by members of a family in everyday interactions.

Language is the main method of human communication. It is expressed by speech, sign, gesture or writing. Language includes receptive skills such as listening and reading, and expressive skills such as speaking and writing. Language is a five-part organized system that includes phonology, syntax, semantics, morphology and pragmatics. Language is physically based, cognitively motivated, emotionally rich and socially shared.

Language loss, also referred to language attrition or language death, refers to the normal and gradual process of first language or L1 decline and eventual forgetting. As contact and use of L1 decreases, proficiency and interest in a new language (most often the majority language) increases leaving speakers with reduced and impoverished L1 proficiency and a gradual shift to the new language.

Language reality refers to a speaker's linguistic situation and includes language skills, use, experiences, exposure and interests.

Language-rich or *multilingual* classrooms are learning spaces filled with languages. In these spaces learners come from different language backgrounds, speak numerous home languages and/or dialects and have various levels of proficiency in the school language.

Language support is the main strategy of multilingual teaching. To support learners' languages means to acknowledge their language abilities, understand their language needs and extend and enrich their language skills and interests.

Learners are students or pupils who engage in acquiring knowledge in an education program.

Linguistically Appropriate Practice or LAP is a multilingual teaching resource developed to integrate and support school language learners.

Linguistically Appropriate Practice PLUS or LAP+ is a multilingual teaching resource developed to support the language interests of school language speakers and bring them into the multilingual teaching agenda.

Manage a language or *master a language* are two general terms that describe stages in language learning. To *manage* a language means to be able to communicate at a basic level, while *mastery* of a language refers to more advanced proficiency and greater communication ability.

Missing piece is the descriptor assigned to school language speakers who are mostly absent from the multilingual teaching agenda.

A *monolingual* is a person who speaks only one language. The productive suffix *-ism* added to monolingual gives us monolingualism which refers to the state or condition of being a single language speaker.

Multilingual teaching is a pedagogy that responds to, supports and extends the language skills, experiences and interests of *all* learners in language-rich classrooms: school language learners *and* school language speakers. This definition stands in stark contrast to the widespread view that multilingual teaching is reserved for only one group of learners, those who are new to the school language.

A *multilingual teaching agenda* or program includes all language-related tasks, activities, topics and strategies that are adopted by teachers to support learners' language skills and interests.

A *native school language speaker* is a learner who acquired the school language (or the language of program delivery) from birth. For native school language speakers the language of the school and the language of the home are the same.

The terms *pedagogy, instructional practice* and *teaching method* all refer to teaching actions, strategies, decisions and plans undertaken, adopted and implemented by teachers.

Proficiency is the ability to perform an action. Language proficiency then, refers to a person's ability to speak a language, perform various language tasks and communicate effectively.

School language, in most cases, is the language of program delivery, and most often the majority or societal language.

School language learners are new to the school language. They are speakers of one or more home languages (or dialects) and add the school language to their language repertoires.

School language speakers are users of the school language. This means that they have some level of ability to understand, share, interact, learn and exchange information in the school language or the language of program delivery. Some school language speakers are former learners of the school language while others are native monolingual speakers for whom the school language is their first and only language.

Translanguage or *translanguaging* is how bi/ multilinguals *language* when they speak with other bi/multilinguals. This means that they mix their languages, strategically select words, terms and speaking and pronunciation styles from their entire language repertoire to navigate and facilitate communication.

The Missing Piece Investigation: Themes and Topics

Theme 1
The Backstory: How it all Happened

Topics

1. **LAP:** Language support for young immigrant children

2. **LAP2:** Language support for school language learners

3. **LAP+:** Language support for school language speakers

Topic 1: Language Support for Young Immigrant Children
Linguistically Appropriate Practice: A Guide for Working with Young Immigrant Children

LAP

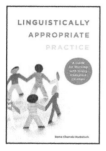

Linguistically Appropriate Practice: A Guide for Working with Young Immigrant Children or LAP (Chumak-Horbatsch, 2012) was published more than 10 years ago in repsonse to numerous requests from early childhood practitioners and primary grade teachers who found it difficult to connect with young *immigrant* children. These educators wanted to know *what works best* with children who do not speak the school language and asked for a guide that would help them integrate these learners into the classroom and the curriculum.

LAP (see image on previous page) proved to be what the early childhood practitioners and teachers asked for. LAP describes a new way to work with young immigrant children, explains their language reality and their unique language and literacy needs. LAP encourages teachers to support and nurture the home languages of these *emergent bilinguals* (García & Kleifgen, 2010), help them learn the school language and respond to their unique dual language needs.

Since its publication, LAP has become the *go to* resource for teachers working with young language learners in Canada, the United States, in European and Nordic countries, Australia and Japan. Used in childcare centres, preschool groups, family literacy groups, kindergartens and primary level (Grades 1–3) classrooms, LAP has also been adapted in specialized programs, such as language teaching and early language intervention. LAP has found its way into professional book clubs and staff meetings. It is shared and discussed at multilingual workshops and conferences. In 2018 LAP was translated into Greek[1] to help teachers integrate young newcomers.

Shortly after the publication of LAP, I set out on a follow-up, fact-finding journey. My purpose was to gauge the response to LAP, evaluate its effectiveness, and identify strengths and areas for improvement. This journey lasted five years and included fieldwork, presentations, publications, the promotion of LAP and the development of an undergraduate LAP course. During that time I collaborated with colleagues, researchers, university students, children, families, authors and school administrators in 15 countries. During my LAP fact-finding journey I recorded all that I witnessed, observed, encountered, heard and overheard. My documentation trove included detailed field notes, photographs, video-clips, audio-recordings, drawings, stories, displays, learners' journals, evaluations and resource lists.

Topic 2: Language Support for School Language Learners
Using Linguistically Appropriate Practice: A Guide for Teaching in Multilingual Classrooms

LAP2

The outcome of my five-year fact-finding journey was an updated version of LAP (Chumak-Horbatsch, 2019) entitled *Using Linguistically Appropriate Practice: A Guide for Teaching in Multilingual Classrooms* (see image) and referred to here as LAP2. Published in late 2019, LAP2 includes reports, testimonials, reflections and comments from more than 30 contributors from seven countries (Canada, Finland, Germany, Iceland, India, Luxembourg and Sweden), who, at the time of writing, were using LAP in various education contexts and levels to support older school language learners. Firmly grounded in bilingual and language learning theories, frameworks and orientations, LAP2 uses a simple tree to explain the theory–practice connection, provides a characterization of the LAP teacher, describes the language-rich classroom, includes suggestions to resolve challenges identified by teachers, and provides a step-by-step implementation guide to support older school language learners.

Topic 3: Language Support for School Language Speakers
Multilingual Teaching: The Missing Piece

LAP+

The discovery of the missing piece in multilingual teaching led to the preparation of the book you are reading. It begins with the identification of school language speakers as the *missing piece* in multilingual teaching and is followed by an investigation of their language reality. It makes a case for acknowledging the rich language lives of this overlooked group of learners and provides a teaching tool especially developed to support their language interests.

Note

(1) Greek translation (2018): Γλωσσικα καταλληλη πρακτικη Ένας οδηγος για εργασια με μικρα παιδια μεταναστων (DiSIGMA Publications: www.disigma.gr).

References

Chumak-Horbatsch, R. (2012) *Linguistically Appropriate Practice: A Guide for Working with Young Immigrant Children.* University of Toronto Press.

Chumak-Horbatsch, R. (2019) *Using Linguistically Appropriate Practice: A Guide for Teaching in Multilingual Classrooms.* Multilingual Matters.

García, O. and Kleifgen, J.A. (2010) *Educating Emergent Bilinguals: Policies, Programs, and Practices for English Language Learners.* Teacher's College Press.

Theme 1 Summary

LAP started out as a guide for teachers working with young immigrant children. Over the years it evolved and changed in a number of important ways. It extended its reach to school language learners across educational levels, and programs. It took on an international scope and is currently adopted by teachers working with school language learners in over 10 countries. When the missing piece in multilingual teaching was discovered, LAP took a new turn, and became LAP+ to welcome school language speakers into the multilingual teaching family.

Theme 2
School Language Speakers: A Language Profile

Topics

1. Who are school language speakers?
2. Former school language learners
3. Native school language speakers

Topic 1: Who are School Language Speakers?

School language speakers are a group of learners in language-rich classrooms who have been identified as the missing piece in multingual teaching and whose language lives and interests remain mostly unknown to teachers who focus on supporting school language learners. As speakers of the school language, these learners remain on the sidelines and rarely participate in multi-language activities. Figure 1 shows two distinct groups of school language speakers: former school language learners and native school language speakers. Let's take a closer look with examples.

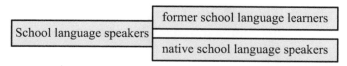

Figure 1 Two distinct groups of school language speakers

Topic 2: Former School Language Learners

Former school language learners were once new to the school language. Having managed or mastered the school language, their status changed from school language *learner* to school *language speaker*. In most language-rich classrooms the number of former school language learners is usually small when compared with learners of the school language. Here are the main features of former school language learners' language reality:

- they have different language backgrounds;
- they were born abroad or in the host country;
- they have home languages (or dialects) that are different from the school language;
- they have a home–school language mismatch;
- initial exposure to the school language is often in the neighbourhood and in school;
- they learn the school language over time;
- the school language is added and they become bilingual;
- over time, proficiency in the school language improves;
- the home language moves to second place;
- they start to prefer the school language;
- the school language becomes more important (dominant);
- the school language is used at home;
- active bilingualism turns to passive bilingualism;

- home language use is reduced; and
- over time, home language loss occurs.

Alvaro: age 7, grade 2

Alvaro was born in Toronto, Canada, into a Portuguese-speaking immigrant family. His first language was Portuguese. At age four, Alvaro attended an English-language full day kindergarten. He spoke Portuguese with a smattering of English words and expressions. By the end of the kindergarten year, however, Alvaro developed basic English language skills and started his Portuguese–English bilingual journey, managing English in school and speaking Portuguese at home. Over the next three years, by age seven, as his English improved, his proficiency in Portuguese weakened. At home, when addressed in Portuguese, Alvaro responded in English and showed little interest in Saturday Portuguese school and in the Portuguese community events his family regularly attended. His language then shifted and English became his dominant language. While Alvaro still understands Portuguese, he is unwilling to use it. His passive bilingualism includes a general understanding of Portuguese and a clear preference for English. If this continues, it is safe to say that Alvaro's Portuguese will further decrease and he will become an English language monolingual.

Topic 3: Native School Language Speakers

Native school language speakers are monolinguals. Their numbers in most language-rich classrooms is small. Unlike former school language learners, information about native school language speakers' language background is sparse. When asked about their language interests, teachers are surprised by the question, and report that these learners have a clear academic advantage because the school language is their *natural and only language*.

Matt: age 10, grade 5

Matt was born in Toronto, Canada and is a native speaker of English. He is in a grade five classroom filled with languages. Most of his classmates are learning English and have one or more home languages or dialects. Some are former language learners, while others, like himself, are native speakers of English. Matt's passion for French comes from his uncle who lives in Montréal[1] and often visits Matt's family in Toronto. Encouraged to learn *la belle langue*, Matt has a small French vocabulary.

When Teacher B (who we will meet in Theme 7) engaged Matt in discussions about language, he was surprised at Matt's high level of language knowledge. He discovered, for example, that Matt had a keen interest in language, an awareness of language differences, an admiration of the home language skills of his classmates, and an interest in different writing systems. When asked about his language experiences beyond English, Matt named friends, neighbors and family friends who spoke different languages. He also described shops with *loud music* in other languages, non-English street signs, bi/multilingual announcements on aeroplanes, movies with subtitles and language options in drop-down menus in computer programs and games. Matt also expressed an interest in learning a new language. When asked which language, he reported one spoken by a friend. When asked about classroom language activities Matt stated that these are for school language learners, not speakers.

In sum

The language stories of Alvaro and Matt show very different language realities. Alvaro's language situation includes single, then dual-language learning, language shift, language repositioning and language loss. His language journey (Figure 2) began with a single (monolingual) home language, Portuguese (Box A). With exposure to English he developed into a Portuguese–English active bilingual (Box B) with two language contexts: Portuguese at home and English at school. Continued exposure to English transformed Alvaro into an English–Portuguese passive bilingual (Box C). His preference for English combined with his negative attitude to all things Portuguese will most likely lead to further loss of Portuguese and result in single language use or English monolingualism (Box D).

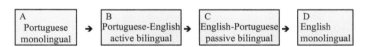

Figure 2 Alvaro's language journey

Three things stand out in the language story of Matt: he lives in a multilingual world, has high levels of language awareness and an organic interest in language. As a speaker of only English, he is surrounded by languages: he learns in a multilingual classroom and lives in a linguistically diverse neighborhood. His daily interactions with classmates who speak different languages provide him with diverse and rich language experiences and a possible *exposure advantage* (Liberman *et al.*, 2017; Fan *et al.*, 2015) that could explain his language awareness and interest.

Note

(1) Montréal is the largest city in Canada's Québec province where French is the official language. Over 75% of residents speak French as their native tongue, and approximately 95% are proficient in the language. See https://en.wikipedia.org/wiki/Montreal.

References

Fan, S.P., Liberman, Z., Keysar, B. and Kinzler, K.D. (2015) The exposure advantage: Early exposure to a multilingual environment promotes effective communication. *Psychological Science* 26 (7), 1090–1097. https://www.doi.org/10.1177/0956797615574699

Liberman, Z., Woodward, A.L., Keysar, B. and Kinzler, K.D. (2017) Exposure to multiple languages enhances communication skills in infancy. *Developmental Science* 20 (1). https://www.doi.org/10.1111/desc.12420

Theme 2 Summary

This theme profiles two distinct groups of school language speakers in language-rich classrooms: former school language learners and native school language speakers. As the two examples show, the language reality of these two groups is quite different. Former school language learners walk in two (or more) language worlds and experience language change and shift, while their monolingual school-language speaking classmates marvel at the languages that surround them and have a natural interest in languages.

Theme 3
LAP+: A New Resource

Topics

1. What is LAP+?
2. Teaching through a LAP+ lens
3. Language engagement strategy
4. LAP+ message to school language speakers

Topic 1: What is LAP+?

LAP+ is a new teaching resource, especially developed to bring school language speakers into the multilingual teaching program and support their language needs and interests. Here are the main features of this new multilingual teaching resource:

- takes multilingual teaching beyond support for school language learners;
- promotes a *no-learner-left-behind* approach to multilingual teaching;
- propels multilingual teaching to a new level of inclusion and equity;
- acknowledges the language richness of school language speakers;
- supports their language skills, experiences and interests;
- helps them better understand their own language lives;

- opens up new language worlds to them;
- helps them reach higher levels of language understanding; and
- fosters and encourages bi/multilingualism.

Topic 2: Teaching through a LAP+ Lens

The term '*teaching through a multilingual lens*' (Cummins & Persad, 2014) is a pedagogical orientation that views the home languages of school language learners as *intellectual resources and personal accomplishments* that are important for academic success. LAP+ widens the scope of the multilingual lens and maintains that the home languages of former school language learners (now speakers of the school language) are no less important than those of their school language learning classmates, and that they too should be viewed as *intellectual resources and personal accomplishments*. For example, LAP+ teachers know that former school language learners will benefit if, like their classmates, they are given the opportunity to negotiate their *identities of competence* (Manyak, 2004), better understand their two language worlds, grow in self-confidence and believe that they too have the potential to grow bilingually.

Topic 3: Language Engagement Strategy

The main strategy of LAP+ is to engage school language speakers in meaningful and relevant language activities. The six-action language engagement plan (see Box on next page) includes preparatory steps, language discussions, activity selection, a question-probe and suggestions for language task assessment. What follows is a brief description of each of the six language engagement actions.

1. Inform families
2. Collect language information
3. Talk about language
4. Select language activities
5. Use the question-probe: *Did you know that…?*
6. Document and assess progress

(1) Inform families

LAP+ teachers inform families that language discovery and exploration plans are in place and that home support, follow-up and encouragement are important to sustain interest and strengthen learning.

(2) Collect language information

Teachers who adopt LAP+ need basic information about the language experiences and interests of school language speakers. This can be obtained by asking families/parents to provide information about language(s) used in the home, proficiency levels and learners' language interests. Another way to collect language information is to directly engage school language speakers in age-appropriate discussions about their language experiences and interests.

(3) Talk about language

Talking about language in an age-appropriate way is an important part of the language engagement strategy. Here are six reasons why:

- strengthens the learner–teacher relationship;
- allows teachers to learn about school language speakers' language skills and interests;

- helps in the planning of language activities;
- sends the message that language is important;
- encourages participation in language activities; and
- extends learners' knowledge about language concepts.

Topics of language discussions can be familiar, factual, newsworthy, controversial, challenging or humorous.[1] They can be teacher-directed and curriculum related, or they can be learner-directed and spontaneous. Language discussions can be one-on-one or in small groups.

(4) Select language activities

Many of the language activities found in the two LAP guidebooks (Chumak-Horbatsch, 2012, 2019) can be offered to school language speakers. They can be used as they appear in the guidebooks, or they can be adapted and adjusted to match the level, ability, interests and needs of school language speakers. To ensure that language activities are meaningful and relevant, teachers can invite school language speakers to choose, and if necessary, modify activities. In addition to the available activities, LAP+ teachers can develop new ways of engaging school language speakers. For example, language discussions often lead to new and creative activity ideas, as we will see in Theme 7.

(5) Use the question-probe: Did you know that …?

This question-probe is an effective way to begin a language discussion. It communicates a genuine interest in learners and is an interesting, at times challenging, way to engage them in language discovery and inquiry. Examples of the *Did you know that…?* question-probe are provided in Theme 7.

(6) Document and assess progress

To track and assess language activity progress, LAP+ adopts *descriptive feedback* or DF, a new interactive assessment tool[2] that includes a proficiency scale showing learners' progress along a continuum from emerging, to developing, to proficient, to extending (Figure 3). Adapted to the learners' level and ability, the DF tool can be used by the teacher, by the learner and/or by both to assess progress and set goals for moving forward. Older learners can self-evaluate and record their progress in a language journal or a language log.

EMERGING (initial)	DEVELOPING (partial)	PROFICIENT (complete)	EXTENDED (advanced)

Figure 3 Levels of understanding of language concepts and competencies

Topic 4: LAP+ Message to School Language Speakers

Engaging school language speakers in language activities sends an inclusive and caring message:

🔊 YOUR LANGUAGE SKILLS AND INTERESTS MATTER!

Included in this general message are the following reminders, invitations, prompts and encouragement:

• *Speaking the school language is by no means the end of your language journey.*

- *You are a capable and competent language learner.*
- *Your language experiences, interests and stories matter.*
- *There is much to know and learn about language.*
- *Your home language/dialect is important.*
- *Forgotten parts of your home language can be relearned.*
- *Bi/multilingualism is a realistic goal for you.*
- *Exploring the school language is important and exciting.*
- *You can learn a new language.*

Notes

(1) See Theme 8: How language works.
(2) Figure 3: Language activity proficiency scale. Adapted from: https://www.prn.bc.ca/board/k-12-reporting-policy-framework-2023-2024/

References

Chumak-Horbatsch, R. (2012) *Linguistically Appropriate Practice: A Guide for Working with Young Immigrant Children.* University of Toronto Press.

Chumak-Horbatsch, R. (2019) *Using Linguistically Appropriate Practice: A Guide for Teaching in Multilingual Classrooms.* Multilingual Matters.

Cummins, J. and Persad, R. (2014) Teaching through a multilingual lens: The evolution of EAL policy and practice in Canada. *Education Matters* 2 (1), 3–40.

Manyak, P.C. (2004) "What did she say?" Translation in a primary-grade English immersion class. *Multicultural Perspectives* 6 (1), 12–18. https://doi.org/10.1207/S15327892mcp0601_3

Theme 3 Summary

LAP+ is a much-needed multilingual teaching resource for language-rich classrooms. It brings school language speakers on board, widens the multilingual teaching lens and tells them that, even though they are speakers of the school language, their language journey is far from over. Rather, they have much to discover and learn about language.

Theme 4
LAP+ Stands Strong

To say that LAP+ stands strong means that this multilingual teaching resource has solid support and backing. The six support pillars described in this theme provide a strong rationale for adopting LAP+ and extending language support to school language speakers. Let's take a closer look at the six support pillars (Figure 4).

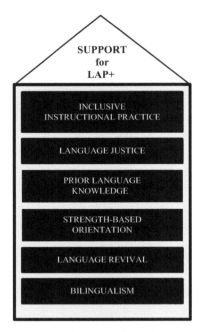

Figure 4 Support for including school language speakers in multilingual teaching

Support Pillar 1: Inclusive Instructional Practice

Directly in line with the principles of inclusive education (Chumak-Horbatsch, 2012, 2019), LAP+ is guided by an *all-in* mandate: open language support to school language speakers.

Support Pillar 2: Language Justice

Language justice, included in the wider concept of social justice (García *et al.*, 2017), is at the heart of LAP+. It is the rationale for including school language speakers in the multilingual teaching agenda and serves as a reminder that the language interests of *all* learners matter. Language justice means that everyone in language-rich classrooms, not only school language learners, has the opportunity to engage in language learning and discovery, make sense of their changing language identities and better understand their language lives.

Support Pillar 3: Prior Language Knowledge

Prior knowledge, experiences and understanding shape learners' identities and play a critical role in new learning (Bransford *et al.*, 2000; Cummins *et al.*, 2005). Stated differently, learners construct new knowledge from what they already know and understand. LAP+ applies this *familiar–new* principle by acknowledging school language speakers' language skills, using them to inform multilingual teaching and helping these learners reach higher levels of language understanding.

Support Pillar 4: Strength-Based Orientation

LAP+ views school language speakers as competent, resourceful and creative language learners, who, like their school language learning classmates, can develop identities of language competence (Manyak, 2004), acquire higher-order language knowledge and become bi/multilingual. LAP+ teachers know that rusty and neglected home languages of former school language learners can be revived and that native school language speakers' organic interest in language can lead to additional language learning.

Support Pillar 5: Language Revival

According to Noam Chomsky,[1] a language can never be totally lost or erased. Monica Schmid (2011), a language loss-revival scholar agrees. *It's still there*, she writes, *just buried and dormant*. Forgotten languages can be revived, reactivated and relearned because much of the acquired knowledge remains in long-term memory (Grosjean, 2004; Fishman, 1991). Knowing this, LAP+ teachers reach out to former school language learners, discuss their home language learning experiences, explain the reality of language revival, provide age-appropriate language learning materials and set them on the path to home language recovery. We will return to this topic in Theme 8 (Topic 13: Forgotten and Lost Languages).

Support Pillar 6: Bilingualism is Better

Bilingualism,[2] or knowing and using more than one language, opens new worlds and shows speakers different ways of talking, singing, cooking, eating, dressing, counting, joking and worshiping. It develops an awareness of language differences, extends learners' understanding of each *other*, improves the ability to problem solve and multi-task. Bilinguals dream in both of their languages, naturally translanguage or mix their two languages and know that translating idioms doesn't work.[3] Research studies over the past 40 years have concluded that compared to monolinguals, bilingual children whose two languages are relatively balanced in proficiency, have increased cognitive and language-processing skills such as classification, problem solving, mental flexibility, early reading, and executive function or mental skills such as the ability to control attention, inhibit distraction, manage sets of stimuli, and shift between tasks (Baker, 2021; Chumak-Horbatsch, 2012, 2019). Aware that bilingualism is a *positive force* (Cummins, 2021), LAP+ teachers encourage former school language learners to return to their home languages and renew and reactivate their bilingualism. And they go one step further: they challenge native school language speakers to tackle a new language.

Notes

(1) https://www.psychologytoday.com/ca/blog/life-bilingual/201207/can-first-language-be-totally-forgotten

(2) See also Theme 8: How Language Works; Topic 9: Bilingualism: Common Myths; Topic 10: Childhood Bilingualism: Common Myths.

(3) An example of idiomatic translation from Italian: The idiom *in bocca al lupo (in the mouth of a wolf)* is widely

used in Italian to wish someone *Good luck*. Used instead of *Buona fortuna (Good luck)* this idiom comes from the Italian superstition that if you wish someone good luck, then unpleasant things will happen. The response to this idiom is not *Grazie* (Thank you), but rather *Crepi il lupo* (May the wolf die). The English equivalent is *break a leg*, which has the same *Good luck* meaning.

References

Baker, C. and Wright, W.E. (2021) *Foundations of Bilingual Education and Bilingualism* (7th edn). Multilingual Matters.

Bransford, J.D., Brown, A.L. and Cocking, R. (2000) *How People Learn: Brain, Mind, Experience, and School.* National Academy Press.

Chumak-Horbatsch, R. (2012) *Linguistically Appropriate Practice: A Guide for Working with Young Immigrant Children.* University of Toronto Press.

Chumak-Horbatsch, R. (2019) *Using Linguistically Appropriate Practice: A Guide for Teaching in Multilingual Classrooms.* Multilingual Matters.

Cummins, J. (2021) *Rethinking the Education of Multilingual Learners: A Critical Analysis of Theoretical Concepts.* Multilingual Matters.

Cummins, J., Bismilla, V., Chow, P., Cohen, S.L., Giampapa, F., Leoni, L., Sandu, P. and Sastri, P. (2005) Affirming identity in multlingual classrooms. *Educational Leadership: Journal of the Department of Supervision and Curriculum Development,* N.E.A. 63 (1), 38–43.

Fishman, J. (1991) *Reversing Language Shift: Theory and Practice of Assistance to Threatened Languages.* Multilingual Matters.

García, O., Flores, N. and Spotti, M. (eds) (2017) *The Handbook of Language and Society.* Oxford University Press.

Grosjean, F. Le bilinguisme et le biculturalisme: quelques notions de base. In C. Billard, M. Touzin and P. Gillet (eds) *Troubles spécifiques des apprentissages: l'état des connaissances.* Paris: Signes Editions.

Manyak, P.C. (2004) "What did she say?" Translation in a primary-grade English immersion class. *Multicultural Perspectives* 6 (1), 12–18.
Schmid, M. (2011) *Language Attrition*. Cambridge University Press.

Theme 4 Summary

The six support pillars presented in this theme serve as a professional green light for teachers to adopt LAP+ and support the language interests of school language speakers. Familiarity with the support pillars will give teachers the confidence to say:

'I support the language interests of school language speakers, here's why …'

Theme 5
The Language-Rich Classroom

Topics
1. What is a language-rich classroom?
2. Language treasure troves
3. Language gardens
4. Democratic spaces
5. The multilingual bridge
6. Classroom language policy
7. Healthy linguistic diet

Topic 1: What is a Language-Rich Classroom?

A language-rich or multilingual classroom is an educational space where learners have different language backgrounds, speak home languages or dialects that are different from the school language and have various levels of proficiency in the school language. Language-rich classrooms include learners who are new to the school language and who have a home–school language mismatch. They also include speakers of the school language. Some are former school language learners who, over the years, have managed or mastered the school language, and continue to experience some level of home–school language mismatch, while others are native speakers of the school language, who are monolingual and for whom the home and the school language is the same.

Topic 2: Language Treasure Troves

Referring to language-rich classrooms as language treasure troves is accurate and *spot on*. The term *treasure trove* (*tresor trové* in French; *il tesoro trovato* in Italian; *скарбниця* in Ukrainian) can be traced back to the Latin expression, *thesaurus inventus*.[1] *Thesaurus* simply means treasure or treasury while *inventus* means *found*, bringing the meaning of *treasure trove* to a discovered treasure. Aware of this linguistic wealth, LAP+ teachers acknowledge, nurture, support and enrich the languages of all learners in language-rich classrooms.

Topic 3: Language Gardens

 Language-rich classrooms are like language gardens (Garcìa, 1986).[2] In the place of plants and flowers, language gardens are spaces filled with different language sounds, rhythms, tones, melodies, behaviors, practices, symbols and signs. Just as real gardeners tend their flowers and plants, provide nourishment, water, rich soil, stakes and protection, LAP+ teachers nurture two groups of language flowers that have traditionally remained out of the sun: former school language learners and native school language speakers. Just as gardeners talk to their flowers and plants to encourage growth and blooms, LAP+ teachers encourage, support and extend the language interests and skills of all school language speakers.

Topic 4: Democratic Spaces

According to the democratic approach to education, language-rich classrooms are more than spaces filled with languages. Rather, they are spaces that rest on four democratic principles: language equality, language freedom, language discussion and language engagement (Collins *et al.*, 2019; Sant, 2019; Dewey, 1916/ 1985). With these principles in place, language-rich classrooms become welcoming, open, fair, safe and risk-free learning spaces, where all learners:

- come to understand and develop their language identities;
- respect the language realities of classmates;
- extend their understanding of language;
- use all of their language skills to navigate school work and social interactions;
- participate in activities that match their language interests and realities; and
- work together to build a dynamic multilingual community.

Topic 5: The Multilingual Bridge

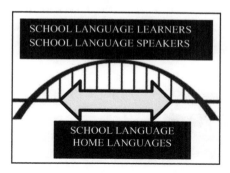

Figure 5 The multilingual bridge

Language-rich classrooms are like bridges (Figure 5) that promote and connect languages. Adapted from Dennis Malone's work on mother tongue-based literacy and multilingual education programs (Malone, 2016: 15), the multilingual bridge is a symbol of inclusive and fair language learning where:

- school language learners freely translanguage or use their entire language repertoire to manage communication and navigate the curriculum (García & Kleyn, 2016; García & Li, 2014; Li, 2016, 2018);
- former school language learners review and revive their home languages; and
- native school language speakers engage in activities that address their language interests and enrich their understanding of language.

Like a real bridge with a secure foundation that supports its entire weight and the loads it will carry, the multilingual bridge stands strong on six support pillars[3] that provide a rationale for adopting LAP+ and extending multilingual teaching to school language speakers.

Topic 6: Classroom Language Policy

To set the tone for an inclusive and respectful language-learning environment, LAP+ teachers begin the school year by engaging learners in an age-appropriate discussion about language, language differences, the school language, home languages and classroom language expectations and behaviors. Using the phrase '*Our classroom is a place where languages are ...*' as a starting point, learners contribute their ideas to create a language roadmap or a classroom language policy (shown on the right). Displayed near the entrance of the classroom, the language policy reminds learners and informs families, staff and visitors that the language-rich classroom is a place where all languages matter.

Topic 7: Healthy Linguistic Diet

It is good for you to eat fruit and vegetables every day.
It is good for you to speak, read and write in different languages.

(Bak & Mehmedbegovic, 2017)

The concept of a *healthy linguistic diet*, or HLD, was introduced more than 10 years ago by two educational researchers (Bak & Mehmedbegovic, 2017) to promote the idea that multiple language learning and use are *key ingredients* in both cognitive development and in one's wellbeing. The authors describe multiple language use as essential mental exercise and a basic need that is just as important as regular physical activity and a healthy diet. They believe that language study should be included in the health education curriculum and caution teachers against the exclusive use of the school language in linguistically diverse classrooms. In line with the HLD concept and the idea that languages are a part of healthy living, LAP+ adds an item to the HLD menu: support the language interests and needs of school language speakers.

Notes

(1) See: https://www.etymonline.com/word/trove
(2) The idea of a language garden was first put forward more than 25 years ago by García (1986).
(3) See also Theme 4: LAP+ Stands Strong.

References

Bak, T.H. and Mehmedbegovic D. (2017) Healthy linguistic diet: The value of linguistic diversity and language learning across the lifespan. *Language, Society & Policy.* https://doi.org/10.17863/CAM.9854

Collins, J., Hess, M.E. and Lowery, C.L. (2019) Democratic spaces: How teachers establish and sustain democracy and education in their classrooms. *Democracy and Education* 27 (1) Article 3.

Dewey, J. (1916/1985) Democracy and education. In J.A. Boydston (ed.) *The Middle Works, 1899–1924* (p. 9). Southern Illinois University Press.

García, O. (1986) *From Language Garden to Sustainable Languaging: Bilingual Education in a Global World.* NABE Perspectives.

García, O. and Kleyn, T. (eds) (2016) *Translanguaging with Multilingual Students: Learning from Classroom Moments.* Routledge.

García, O. and Li, W. (2014) *Translanguaging: Language Bilingualism and Education.* Palgrave Macmillan.

Li, W. (2016) Multi-competence and the translanguaging instinct. In V. Cook and Li, W. (eds) *The Cambridge Handbook of Multi-Competence* (pp. 533–543). Cambridge University Press.

Li, W. (2018) Translanguaging as a practical theory of language. *Applied Linguistics* 39 (1), 9–30.

Malone, D. (2016) What is the most effective approach to transition to the use of a second language as medium of instruction when classroom policy and practice has used the learner's home language/first language in the early primary years? Which school year is best for implementing this transition? In B. Trudell and C. Young (eds) *Good Answers to Tough Questions in Mother Tongue-Based Multilingual Education* (pp. 15–20). SIL International.

Sant, E. (2019) Democratic education: A theoretical review (2006–2017). *Review of Educational Research* 89 (5). https://doi.org/10.3102/0034654319862493

Theme 5 Summary

Language-rich classrooms are linguistically healthy places, where:

- all languages are included, nurtured and supported;
- all learners grow and thrive linguistically;
- a collectively prepared language policy helps sustain a positive and inclusive language learning environment.

Theme 6
LAP+ Teachers

Topics
1. Who are LAP+ teachers?
2. Languagekeepers
3. Language role models
4. Language profiles
5. Connecting theory to practice
6. Multilingual teaching activism
7. Chief (language) opportunity orchestrators

Topic 1: Who are LAP+ Teachers?

LAP+ teachers are committed to fully inclusive and linguistically fair teaching. They know that all learners, not only those learning the school language, have rich language lives and unique language stories to share. For this reason they welcome school language speakers into the multilingual teaching agenda, and support their language interests by adopting the language engagement strategy.[1]

Topic 2: Languagekeepers

Keeper is an interesting word. Traced back to the 13th century it is an agent noun from the verb *to keep* and is defined as *one who has charge of some person or thing, a warden, protector or custodian*.[2] Today the word *keeper* can be found in many English compound words, such as: *goalkeeper, housekeeper, peacekeeper, zookeeper, bookkeeper* and *timekeeper*. In the past, *keeper* was used to refer to a specialist who was responsible for a specific museum collection. Today, museum *keepers* are called *curators* (from the Latin word *cura*, to care for). We take the liberty here to coin a a new compound word, *languagekeeper*, to describe LAP+ teachers who support, nurture and protect the language interests of all learners.

Topic 3: Language Role Models

As language role models, LAP+ teachers influence and shape learners' language understanding, attitudes, interests and behaviors. The things they say and do and the encouragement they provide inspire language discovery and help learners:

- develop positive attitudes towards language;
- remain open and receptive to language differences;
- view language variation as both an asset and a bonus;
- develop an interest in additional language learning;
- understand the benefits of multiple perspectives;
- collaborate and learn from each other; and
- view bilingualism as a realistic and reachable goal.

Topic 4: Language Profiles

Like learners in language-rich classrooms, LAP+ teachers have rich and varied language skills, interests and experiences. Some are monolingual or speakers of only the school language, others use two languages (or dialects) in their daily lives and are bilingual, while others navigate three (or more) languages and are multilingual (see Figure 6). LAP+ teachers have valuable language experiences connected with relationships, family, interests, hobbies, travel and/or study. Some are learning a new language while others are reviving a neglected one. Many teachers prepare for travel by downloading and learning *Essential Travel Phrases* and many read novels and watch movies in their home language.

TEACHERS' LANGUAGES
Monolinguals or speakers of only the school language
Bilinguals or speakers of two languages: the school language + one other language (e.g. a home language)
Multilinguals or speakers of more than two languages: the school language + two other language (e.g. home languages)

Figure 6 Teachers' languages

While teachers' language skills and experiences are rarely acknowledeged or considered relevant, LAP+ teachers include them in the multilingual agenda. They know that strategic sharing of their language lives with learners is important. Here are 10 reasons why:

- sends a positive message about home languages;
- provides a positive home language role model;
- presents home languages as important;
- helps learners understand that home languages are part of a speaker's identity;
- improves teacher–learner relationships;
- promotes acceptance of others;
- helps learners connect with the teacher as a language user;
- supports school language learners who share a teacher's home language(s);
- comforts and consoles young learners who are new to the school language; and
- inspires former schoool language learners to revive their neglected or forgotten home languages.

Topic 5: Connecting Theory to Practice

To illustrate how LAP+ teachers connect theory to practice we go to Loris Malaguzzi, *the great Italian educationalist* (Cagliari *et al.*, 2016; Vecchi, 2010). Best known for his role in the development of the Reggio Emilia educational philosophy, Malaguzzi strongly believed that to make teaching relevant and effective, teachers must push on both the practice and the theory pedals of their symbolic teaching *bici* or bicycle.[3] Working only one of the pedals, Malaguzzi believed, will not result in effective teaching.

Applying Malaguzzi's bicycle metaphor to all-inclusive multilingual teaching, we see LAP+

teachers connect practice to theory by working both pedals of the multilingual teaching *bici*. While the practice pedal includes commitment to support the language interests of school language speakers, the adoption of the language engagement strategy, and a general understanding of how language works,[4] the theory pedal of the multilingual teaching *bici* includes familiarity with the six support pillars[5] that explain why school language speakers belong in the multilingual teaching agenda.

Topic 6: Multilingual Teaching Activism

As champions of inclusive and equitable pedagogy, some LAP+ teachers are taking multilingual teaching beyond the classroom. They organize and attend workshops and meetings and advocate the inclusion of school language speakers in the multilingual teaching agenda. Here's an example.

Browsing in the Manchester (UK) Museum Gallery Shop a number of years ago, an unusual card (shown on the left) caught my eye. I bought it, brought it home and set out to discover its creator, history and purpose. I did not realize it at the time, but that card had relevance for multilingual teaching activism. Here's what I discovered.

The creator of the card is Patrick Brill, a British contemporary artist with an unusual pseudonym, Bob and Roberta Smith or BRS. BRS is a writer, author, musician and an arts education activist. He is associate professor at Sir John Cass Department of Art, Media and Design at London Metropolitan University. His bold, expressive and colourful texts, painted on canvas, wood and cardboard, are political statements. I also discovered that the card I purchased was part of a campaign for improved arts education in England launched by BRS in 2013. This campaign was an expression of opposition to the proposed removal of art from the GCSE (General Certificate of Secondary Education) core curriculum. Introducing BRS some time ago, Anna O'Sullivan, director and chief curator (or keeper) of the Butler Gallery in Kilkenny, Ireland, described him as someone who *stirs things up and encourages a response*, an artist who *incites and inspires* and *rallies us to really think about the world we live in*.[6]

BRS did indeed stir, incite, inspire and encourage me. He also provoked me to think about multilingual teaching in a new way. I looked at the card through a fully inclusive lens and saw a multilingual teaching activism resource. I then contacted BRS and explained my purpose: to adjust his message to advocate the inclusion of school language speakers in multilingual teaching. The next day BRS's response arrived: '*Do go ahead*', he generously wrote back.

I shared my museum finding and the subsequent approval from BRS with a group of teachers who had recently started engaging school language speakers in language activities. The teachers googled BRS and found his work (and his hats) captivating.[7] The idea of modifying his arts education poster into a call for fully inclusive multilingual teaching was met with enthusiasm and excitement. The outcome of our work was a somewhat patchy reworked poster (see image on previous page) to encourage teachers working in language-rich classrooms to do five things:

- acknowledge the rich language lives of school language speakers;
- provide them with language learning opportunities;
- make the school language a topic of study and discovery;
- make bi/multilingualism a realistic goal for all learners; and
- share information and resources.

Topic 7: Chief (Language) Opportunity Orchestrators

Some readers may consider the word *orchestrator* an unusual and even strange way to describe teachers. Yet American educator, Chris Aviles, thinks otherwise. He coined the term *Chief Opportunity Orchestrator* or **COO** to describe teachers as arrangers who *create as many opportunities as possible for students and then 'get out of* their way'.[8] We borrow this term from Aviles, sneak the word *language* into COO and refer to LAP+ teachers as *Chief Language Opportunity Orchestrators* or CLOOs, who create language-learning opportunities for school language speakers; provide them with multilingual resources and choices; guide language exploration and discovery and encourage collaboration and sharing.

Notes

(1) See Theme 3, Topic 3: Language Engagement Strategy.
(2) See https://www.etymonline.com/word/keeper
(3) The Italian word *bici* is a contraction of the noun *bicicletta* (bicycle), just as in English, the word *bicycle* is shortened to *bike*.
(4) See Theme 8: How Language Works.
(5) See Theme 4: LAP+ Stands Strong.
(6) See https://adiarts.ie/organisations/partnerships/butler-gallery/art-makes-children-powerful/
(7) See https://en.wikipedia.org/wiki/Bob_and_Roberta_Smith
(8) See https://www.techedupteacher.com/being-the-guide-on-the-side-is-not-enough-become-the-coo/

References

Cagliari, P., Castagnetti, M., Giudici, C., Rinaldi, C., Vecchi, V. and Moss, P. (eds) (2016) *Loris Malaguzzi and the Schools of Reggio Emilia: A Selection of his Writings and Speeches, 1945–1993*. Routledge.

Vecchi, V. (2010) *Art and Creativity in Reggio Emilia: Exploring the Role and Potential of Ateliers in Early Childhood Education*. Routledge.

Theme 6 Summary

As champions of fully inclusive and linguistically fair teaching, LAP+ teachers care for and nurture learners' languages, serve as language role models, strategically share their language experiences, skillfully ride their multilingual teaching *bici*, advocate fully inclusive multilingual teaching and create language-learning opportunities for school language speakers.

Theme 7
LAP+ in Action

Teachers break new ground when they bring school language speakers into the multilingual teaching agenda, a pedagogy that is traditionally reserved for school language learners. This theme describes how two teachers took this innovative pedagogical step, adopted LAP + , and implemented the language engagement strategy to linguistically challenge, motivate and engage two school language speakers.

Topics

1. Alvaro's engagement in language activities
2. Matt's engagement in language activities
3. Benefits of engaging in language activities
4. Assessment

Topic 1: Alvaro's Engagement in Language Activities

We first met Alvaro in Theme 2 (Topic 2) and saw how this former English language learner journeyed from Portuguese monolingualism to active Portuguese–English bilingualism to passive English–Portuguese bilingualism. We saw his growing preference for English (the school language) and his reduced interest in Portuguese, his home language.

Alvaro's initial interest in language activities was minimal. Yet, with encouragement and numerous language-related informal chats with Teacher A, Alvaro engaged in the following six language activities:

(a) Question-probe: *Did you know that one of the best soccer players in the world is Portuguese?*
(b) Flags: selected from the LAP guidebook (Chumak-Horbatsch, 2012: 109–110).
(c) Self-text activity adapted from Cummins and Early (2012).
(d) and (e) Two book activities selected and planned with the assistance of the school librarian.
(f) Question-probe: *Did you know that Duo speaks Portuguese?*

Let's talk about language

Teacher A began her language engagement plan by asking Alvaro about his use of Portuguese in the home. When Alvaro showed a lack of interest, Teacher A pulled out the '*Did you know …?*' question-probe strategy from her teaching toolbox.

(a) Did you know that one of the best soccer players in the world is Portuguese?

This question-probe spoke to Alvaro's love of soccer. He responded immediately by announcing, *Yea, Cristiano Ronaldo plays for the Portuguese national soccer team.* With the help of his older brother, Alvaro created an English–Portuguese soccer word list that he shared with Teacher A and read the words and phrases in both languages.

He explained that the word for soccer in Portuguese is *futebol*, but that it is not the same as American football. The difference, he explained, is in the shape of ball: *round* for soccer and *long* for football. At this point Teacher A stepped in and, changing the question-probe, extended the activity by asking Alvaro: *I wonder what the long football shape is called?*

(b) The flags of my two countries: Canada and Portugal

Alvaro participated in the flag activity and created two flags: Canadian and Portuguese.[1]

(c) Self-text

Knowing that Alvaro had a unique language story, Teacher A encouraged him to create a self-text or a personal account of his dual language experiences. The open nature of this activity gave Alvaro a choice in materials, format and time frame. Guided by Teacher A, Alvaro decided to call his text '*My language story*'. He started by drawing all the members of his family. To each he added a caption (in English) indicating which language or languages they speak. Under his image he wrote English and Portuguese. '*Ah*', said Teacher A, '*Did you know that you're bilingual!*' She explained that a bilingual is someone who knows and uses two languages. To this Alvaro replied: '*Yea, I'm bilingual*'. The activity found its way to Alvaro's home where his brother helped him add information about their relatives in the Azores.

(d) Book activity #1

Teacher A introduced Alvaro to a Portuguese–English dual-language e-book (shown on the right) with a catchy and amusing title: *Os extraterrestres adoram cuecas* (*Aliens love underpants*). This silly story explains that Aliens come to planet Earth

because there are no underpants in space. On planet Earth, Aliens find all shapes and sizes of underpants drying on washing lines. With the help of his older brother, Alvaro read the book at home. Back in the classroom, he described the experience as *fun and filled with Portuguese words*.

(e) Book activity #2

Alvaro loved *Nimoshom and his Bus* (Thomas, 2017: shown on the left), a story read to the class by the school librarian.[2] This short and simple story, with delightful illustrations, introduced Alvaro and his grade two classmates to Cree, an indigenous language. *Nimoshom* (which means grandfather in Cree) is the driver of a school bus. He speaks Cree with the children he drives to school, telling them *tansi, tansi* (hello) or *kinapi, kinapi* (hurry up) or *api, api* (sit down). *Nimoshom* tells stories and makes the children laugh. When the children get off the bus, *Nimoshom* does not say *goodbye*, because most Cree speakers do not use this parting word.

Instead, he says *ekosi, ekosi*, which means *Okay, that's it*.

Two things motivated Alvaro to explore the Cree language: the Cree–English bilingual list of words used by *Nimoshom* found in the back of the book and the fact that there are many Cree speakers in Canada. Alvaro created a profile of Cree that he shared with the class. In it he included the following facts:

- a language of the Algonquian group of Indigenous people;
- spoken across Canada;
- the largest Indigenous group in Canada;
- most Cree speakers live in the western provinces: Alberta, Saskatchewan and Manitoba;
- Cree uses symbols but can also be written in letters.

Teacher A praised Alvaro's work and told him that he was somewhat of an expert on the Cree language, a comment that made him very proud.

(f) Did you know that Duo speaks Portuguese?[3]

When Alvaro was introduced to Duolingo, his Portuguese heart was stirred. Duolingo is a free, game-based and fun-filled language-learning tool that, according to its creators, *really works*. The short lessons are guided by Duo, a charming green owl (shown on the left) who loves and promotes languages. After meeting Duo, Alvaro committed to online learning of Portuguese with Duolingo. He worked at home and also in the classroom. The short, animated sessions helped reawaken his Portuguese. As he progressed through the levels, he was both surprised and delighted that Portuguese was *still in his head*.

Topic 2: Matt's Engagement in Language Activities

A native speaker of English, Matt is interested in French, has an organic interest in language, is aware of the language skills of his classmates and has a curiosity about learning a new language. With the encouragement and guidance of Teacher B, Matt participated in five language activities.

(a) Classroom glossary.
(b) *Bon Appétit*: selected from the LAP guidebook (Chumak-Horbatsch, 2012: 127).
(c) Question-probe: *Did you know that English is a global language?*
(d) Question-probe: *Did you know that English is the language of the skies?*
(e) Classroom English-language ambassador.

Let's talk about language

Teacher B introduced Matt to a colorful and age-appropriate book about language. *Chitchat: Celebrating the World's Languages* (Jude, 2013) is an award-winner that has *everything a young reader would ever want to know about language*.

(a) Classroom glossary

When Matt discovered the 22-word *glossary* on page 45 of the *Chitchat* book, he wanted to know more about word lists. He decided to create a *glossary* that would list classroom words and terms. After discussing the main features of a *glossary* with Teacher B (words that are specific to a subject or topic, identified, defined, marked in the singular and alphabetically ordered), he created a list of 27 classroom words and proudly stated that his list was longer than the *glossary* in the *Chitchat* book:

backpack, blackboard, book, bulletin board, ceiling, chair, chalk, chart, clock, coatroom, computer, desk, door, eraser, floor, globe, glue, keyboard, lights, mouse, paint, pencil, scissors, student, teacher, white board, window

(b) *Bon Appétit*

Matt selected the *Bon Appétit* activity because he had heard this meal-time salutation from his uncle who lives in Montréal, and also in the French language classroom (Chumak-Horbatsch, 2012: 127). Surprised that there is no English equivalent for *Bon appétit*, Matt had great fun creating English translations such as *Good appetite! Enjoy! Enjoy eating everybody! Mmmm … C'mon dig in!* It was at this point that Teacher B stepped in with a question-probe: *Did you know that there are other French phrases used in English?* The list provided by Teacher B was shared with the class and also with the French language teacher.[4] While some of the phrases were unknown, everyone agreed that the following four were commonly used: *au revoir, en route, bon voyage* and *papier mâché*.

(c) *Did you know that English is a global language?*

Teacher B challenged Matt with the above question-probe. He encouraged Matt to go on a fact-finding mission, define *global*, find synonyms or words that mean the same, list basic facts about the English language and share his findings with the class. Matt visited English language sites and gathered facts. He included a definition of *global* and found two synonyms: *universal* and *worldwide*. To these he added his personal explanation: *Global really means everywhere*. He used a world map to show the many countries where English is spoken. He shared an important fact that made his fellow native speakers of English proud: English is a language with 1.5 to 2 billion speakers worldwide. He explained terms such as *pronunciation*, *accent* and *dialect* to explain language variation. When Matt shared a YouTube clip of the varieties of English, his classmates were captivated and attempted the pronunciation of words and phrases in Australian and British English.

(d) Did you know that English is the language of the skies?

Table 1 Aviation alphabet

A = Alpha	H = Hotel	O = Oscar	V = Victor
B = Bravo	I = India	P = Papa	W = Whiskey
C = Charlie	J = Juliet	Q = Quebec	X = X-Ray
D = Delta	K = Kilo	R = Romeo	Y = Yankee
E = Echo	L = Lima	S = Sierra	Z = Zulu
F = Foxtrot	M = Mike	T = Tango	
G = Golf	N = November	U = Uniform	

This question-probe piqued Matt's interest and he set out to discover more. He searched the internet and discovered that all pilots in the world are multilingual. This means that they are speakers of English, know additional languages and use the *aviation alphabet* (Table 1) to communicate with other pilots. This activity became both meaningful and personal to Matt. In his presentation he shared what he had learned, showed a YouTube clip entitled '*Language*

Secrets Only Pilots Know[5] and proudly announced: '*I'm going to be a pilot. I already speak English and now all I have to do is learn the Aviation Alphabet and probably some other languages.*'

(e) Classroom English-language ambassador

Teacher B invited Matt to take on the role of classroom English-language ambassador. Working together, they defined the role and listed five responsibilities:

- serve as a representative of the English language;
- collaborate and share facts about the English language;
- respond to questions or concerns about the English language;
- support classmates who are learning English; and
- help classmates find resources for English-language projects.

Topic 3: Benefits of Engaging in Language Activities

Participating in language activities was meaningful and rewarding for both Alvaro and Matt. It gave them a sense of belonging, enjoyment and importance. It changed their role from observer of language activities to active participant, extended their understanding of language concepts, helped them better understand their own language circumstance, developed their communication and collaboration skills and fostered an openness to others. In addition to these general benefits, participation in language activities provided Alvaro and Matt with personal language benefits as shown in Table 2.

Table 2 Benefits for Alvaro and Matt

Benefits for Alvaro: former school language learner
• renewed interest in Portuguese • new skills in Portuguese • step closer to Portuguese-English active bilingualism • new awareness of his Portuguese–English identity • interest in a new language

Benefits for Matt: native school language speaker
• increased language awareness • increased understanding of the English language • interest in language study (French and English) • leadership role: English-language ambassador • interest in additional language learning

Topic 4: Assessment

Alvaro and Matt recorded their language activities in their *Language Logbooks*. Entries included activity name, start and end dates, materials and resources used, and activity response-reflection. In addition to this self-documentation, Teachers A and B provided Alvaro and Matt with *descriptive feedback*.[6] They identified progress and mastery points (emerging, developing, proficient, extending) and, working together, set new goals for moving language learning forward.

Notes

(1) Flags of the world: https://flagpedia.net/index
(2) Mandatory Indigenous-focused learning is part of the Ontario Social Studies curriculum. See https://news. ontario.ca/en/release/1000904/ ontario-to-strengthen-mandatory-indigenous-learning-in-school-curriculum

(3) Duolingo: https://www.duolingo.com/course/pt/en/Learn-Portuguese

(4) French, an official language in Canada, is taught in English-language schools as a second language (FSL) from Grades 4 to 8. For French phrases used in English, see: https://www.englishclub.com/vocabulary/fw-french-phrases.php

(5) 'Language Secrets Only Pilots Know': https://www.youtube.com/watch?v=jCB7-GJeGas

(6) See Theme 3, Topic 3 (no. 6).

References

Chumak-Horbatsch, R. (2012) *Linguistically Appropriate Practice: A Guide for Working with Young Immigrant Children.* University of Toronto Press.

Cummins, J. and Early, M. (2011) *Identity Texts: The Collaborative Creation of Power in Multilingual Schools.* Trentham Books.

Jude, I. (2013) *Chitchat: Celebrating the World's Languages.* Kids Can Press.

Thomas, P. (2017) *Nimoshom and his Bus.* Highwater Press. Treaty 1 Territory, homeland of the Métis Nation.

Theme 7 Summary

In this theme we saw how LAP+ plays out in real classrooms with real school language speakers. Participation in language activities was a positive and enjoyable experience for Alvaro, a former English language learner and Matt, a native speaker of English. Both boys were rewarded for their engagement in the language activities. Benefits included a higher level of language knowledge and a sharper awareness of their own language circumstance. Evaluation and progress of language activities was a task shared by teacher and learner.

Theme 8
How Language Works

The title of this last theme comes from an extraordinary book: *How Language Works: How Babies Babble, Words Change Meaning and Languages Live or Die*, written by the renowned linguist and language lover, David Crystal (2007). This book is the go-to resource for teachers working in language-rich classrooms. The following review of *How Language Works* says it all:

> *In this fascinating survey of everything from how sounds become speech to how names work, David Crystal answers every question you might ever have had about the nuts and bolts of language in his usual highly illuminating way. Along the way we find out about eyebrow flashes, whistling languages, how parents teach their children to speak, how politeness travels across languages and how the way we talk shows not just how old we are but where we're from and even who we want to be.*[1]

Understanding how language works is important for teachers working in language-rich classrooms. In a general sense, understanding language is part of a broad knowledge of the world, similar to knowledge about addition and subtraction, world geography, famous people and the solar system (Wong-Fillmore & Snow, 2000). On a personal level, language knowledge helps in the understanding of one's language experiences. In a professional sense, familiarity with language, facts, concepts and truths helps teachers:

- support and guide multilingual teaching;
- plan a language program;
- respond to learners' language questions and concerns;
- inspire language discovery and learning;
- encourage additional language learning; and
- ignite interest in *all things* language.

Topics

1. Language and speech
2. The origins of language: theories and sources
3. Language: fast facts
4. World languages: facts, numbers and truths
5. Dialects
6. Our multilingual world
7. Bi/multilingualism is good for us
8. Bilingual dogs
9. Bilingualism: Common myths
10. Childhood bilingualism: Common myths
11. Translate or interpret?
12. Sign language
13. Forgotten and lost languages
14. Language celebrations
15. Language resources

The 15 topics included in this theme come from the many questions, observations and comments I have received over the years from teachers and learners in language-rich classrooms. Readers are encouraged to strategically weave the language topics found here into their multilingual teaching agenda, use the *Did you know that ...?* question-probe and help learners extend their understanding of language and language concepts.[2]

Topic 1: Language and Speech

Language is the main method of human communication. It is expressed by speech, gesture, sign or writing. Language is an organized, rule-governed, five part-system:

- Phonology refers to the sounds and sound combinations within a language.
- Syntax is the arrangement of words and phrases to create well-formed sentences.
- Semantics refers to meanings associated with words and phrases.
- Morphology is the study of word formations.
- Pragmatics is the study of how meaning is constructed in social contexts.

Language is dynamic. This means that it is constantly changing, evolving and adapting to the needs of speakers. Language is also subjective. The way it is used reflects a speaker's identity, culture and, at times, values. Language allows us to share our ideas and thoughts with others. It is a tool that we use to interact with the world around us. Language includes both receptive and expressive skills. Receptive language skills include listening, understanding and reading, while expressive skills include speaking and writing.

Speech: It takes about 100 muscles to speak!

 If language is a system, then speech is a physical activity. To speak means to talk, to utter words, to articulate speech sounds with the ordinary voice and to communicate thoughts and feeling. Speaking is a complex physical process that involves air, vibration and extensive muscle use. The production of speech involves three bodily systems (respiratory, larynx, articulatory) that are regulated on the conscious and the unconscious levels by the nervous system. The vocal apparatus involved in speaking includes lips, tongue, teeth, top of the mouth and the voice box found in the throat. There are muscles in the lips, tongue and throat as well as the cheeks and jaw. It takes about 100 muscles to speak or produce spoken language (Berko Gleason & Bernstein Ratner, 2022).

Topic 2: The Origins of Language: Theories and Sources

How and when did spoken language begin? How and when did first words emerge?

Q A

The short and fast answer to these questions is that *no one really knows*. The long answer is interesting and deserves our attention. According to

Ferretti *et al.* (2018), researchers investigating the origins of language face an *inescapable truth*: because language leaves no trace, the study of the origins of language cannot rely on empirical evidence and remain theoretical and speculative.

Evolutionary and non-evolutionary theories

Continuity or evolutionary (Darwinian) theories work from the assumption that language has such complexity that it could not have developed from nothing. It must have, therefore, evolved from some established earlier pre-linguistic system such as animal communication. The innate position supports this theory and describes language as a species-specific module in the human mind.

Discontinuity or anti-evolutionary theories, on the other hand, claim that language is unique among communication systems and that it must have appeared rather suddenly during human evolution. The culturalist position supports this theory and views language as a cultural system that is learned and acquired through interaction with others (Ulbaek, 1998). Here are seven early theories about the origin of language.

The bow-wow theory

In 1861, Friedrich Max Müller, a German scholar and philologist (one who studies language) proposed that human speech originated from animal sounds. Over time, he argued, mimicked animal sounds evolved into more complex language structures. For example, a dog would be referred to as a *bow-wow* and a cow, a *moo*. Such imitations, called onomatopoeia, do indeed account for a small number of words in many languages and are common in the single-word stage of children's language.

The ding-dong theory

The ding-dong theory also comes from Friedrich Max Müller. This theory holds that the beginnings of spoken language can be found in the human innate sense of rhythm that is related to a flowing universe. Like the *bow-wow theory*, this language origin theory calls on human imitation, not of sound, but of movement. For example, observing a certain rhythm in the world, like the swaying of trees or the sound of a stream, early humans reacted or *ding-donged* phonetically by producing sounds or oral gestures (Crystal, 2005: 351). From these (the thinking goes), a rhythmical hum or chant, in step with natural stimuli, gradually developed into speech sounds.

The yo-he-ho theory

Spoken language arose because early humans worked together. Their physical efforts were accompanied by *communal, rhythmical grunts* (Crystal, 2005: 351). Over time, these grunts evolved into chants and then words such as *heave* and *haul*.

The Tower of Babel theory

The Tower of Babel theory, based on the *city and the tower* narrative found in the Bible,[3] explains why people speak different languages. According to the tale, the world was once monolingual and all people spoke the same language. To avoid a second great flood, a plan was put in place to build a city with a tower high enough to reach heaven. God saw this as human pride and divided people into separate linguistic groups. Unable to understand one another, the construction of the Tower was stopped and people separated into different nations, which is why different countries have different languages.

The pooh-pooh theory

This theory traces spoken language back to emotional, instinctive or involuntary exclamations evoked by pain, surprise, wonder, disapproval and pleasure, such as *ooh! ow!* and *bah!* The universality of these exclamations is used as evidence for this theory.

The gesture theory

The gesture theory focuses on manual signs. The earliest method of human communication, it claims, was by hand sign and gesture. According to Gillespie-Lynch (2017), the early communicative gestures of our ancestors were intentional and purposeful and were accompanied by uncontrolled vocalizations. Over time, tool-use expanded keeping hands busy and occupied, the vocal tract evolved, vocalizations became more controlled and gradually evolved into spoken words.

The la-la theory

> ... *there once was a time when all speech was song, or rather when these two actions were not yet differentiated* ... (Jespersen, 1849: 343)

Attributed to Danish linguist Otto Jespersen (1849), the *la-la theory*, also referred to as the *sing-song theory*, claims that speech originated in song, play, laughter, poetry, courtship and other romantic behaviors. This theory argues that first words were emotional, musical and extended grunt-like calls and cries.

Topic 3: Language: Fast Facts[4]

- There are over 7,000 languages worldwide and most of them are dialects.
- Some languages have millions of speakers and others have only a few.
- About 2,400 of the world's languages are in danger of becoming extinct.
- One language becomes extinct every two weeks.
- An artificial language is created for a particular purpose, rather than one that has developed naturally for purposes of communication.
- There are over 200 artificial languages in books, movies and television shows.
- Only 23 of the world's 7,000 languages are used by more than half of the world's population.
- Due to diversity and immigration, languages of the world influence each other.
- On average, people only use a few hundred words in daily conversation, while most languages have more than 50,000 words.

Topic 4: World Languages: Facts, Numbers and Truths[5]

- Mandarin Chinese is the most spoken language in the world.

- About two-thirds of all languages are from Asia and Africa.
- There are 476 million Indigenous people around the world across more than 90 countries.
- There are more than 4,000 Indigenous languages.
- Indigenous people represent about 5% of the world's population.
- South Africa has 11 official languages.
- Some African languages include clicks or sounds, articulated by suction in the mouth to produce popping, smacking or sucking sounds.
- The three most translated books in the world are: the Bible, *Le Petit Prince* (Antoine de Saint-Exupéry) and *The Adventures of Pinocchio* (Carlo Collodi).
- There are about 24 official languages spoken throughout Europe.
- Over 300 languages are spoken in London, England.
- The United States has no official language.
- After Mexico, the United States has the second-highest number of Spanish speakers.
- The English language contains the most words, with over 250,000.
- The language of airline travel is English using a special Aviation alphabet.
- Other than English, French is the only language taught in every country.
- Cooking and ballet use mostly French words and terms.
- Musical notation is a universal language that musicians worldwide can understand, regardless of their language backgrounds.

- Italian words are used in musical notation to add detailed descriptions for players to understand precisely how the music should be performed: e.g. *adagio, vivace, forte, pianissimo*.
- Music and language are intertwined in our neural networks, suggesting a deep, intrinsic connection.
- Over 20,000 new French words are created each year.
- About 30% of English words come from French.
- After Paris, Kinshasa, the capital city of the Democratic Republic of Congo, is the world's second-largest French-speaking city.
- French is known worldwide as the most romantic language.
- Cambodian has the longest alphabet with 74 characters.
- The Papuan language of Rotokas has only 11 letters, making it the smallest alphabet.
- The Florentine dialect was chosen as the national language of Italy.
- Most regions in Italy speak their dialects.
- Italian is a minority language in Brazil.
- At a language competition in Italy, Ukrainian was recognized as the second most melodic language in the world (after Italian).
- The first printed book was in German.
- The four most spoken languages in Europe are Russian, followed by German, then French and English.
- German words have three genders: masculine, feminine, and neuter. Most languages have only two.
- Papua New Guinea has the most languages, 840.

- The languages spoken in North Korea and South Korea are different. They have distinct vocabularies and grammatical rules due to their many years of separation.
- Spanish is the second most spoken language in the world.
- Twenty-one countries have Spanish as their official language.
- Spanish contains about 4,000 Arabic words.
- The Pope tweets in nine languages, but his Spanish account has the most followers.
- The language of La Gomera, off the coast of Spain, consists entirely of whistles.
- Russian was the first language spoken in outer space.
- Hindi didn't become the official language of India until 1965.
- Japanese uses three different writing systems: Kanji, Katakana and Hiragana.

Topic 5: Dialects

A dialect is a specific form of a standard language. It is like a compass that signals where a speaker comes from (regional dialect), the speaker's social background (class dialect) and/or the speaker's occupation (occupational dialect). A dialect follows many of the rules of the standard language, but also has its own vocabulary, grammar and pronunciation. While all languages have dialects, it is difficult to definitively say how many dialects there are in the world. This is because linguists often disagree as to the definition of a separate and distinct language and that of a dialect. Here are some examples: English has about 160 dialects. Of all the international English dialects, American English has the most speakers. The three Chinese dialects, often referred to as separate languages, are Mandarin, Cantonese and Hakka. Germany has approximately 250 dialects, Italy, over 30, and India has over 1,000.

Some dialects are mutually intelligible, which means that dialect speakers can understand other dialect speakers without any prior knowledge or effort, or they are mutually unintelligible where dialect speakers cannot understand other dialect speakers due to significant pronunciation and vocabulary differences.

Even though dialects are often viewed negatively and seen as sub-standard varieties of a language spoken only by lower-status groups, it is important to remember that dialects express speakers' identity and also the unique characteristics of a particular region. There are promising research findings about children's use of two dialects. For example, two recent studies (Antoniou & Katsos, 2017; Antoniou *et al*., 2020) found that bi-dialectalism, or speaking two dialects of the same language, a widespread practice found in many parts of the world, *trains the brain in the same way as bilingualism*. This means that the human mind does not significantly differentiate between dialects and language, and that children who speak two dialects share similar cognitive advantages, as children who speak two different languages. The authors of these studies conclude that dialects are under-recognized and undervalued and that bi-dialectalism is as advantageous as bilingualism.

Topic 6: Our Multilingual World

> *Speaking two or more languages is the natural way of life for three-quarters of the human race.*
>
> (Crystal, 2007: 409)

- Multilingualism is defined as the presence and use of more than two languages.
- Multilingualism exists on two levels: individual (personal) and societal.
- Societal multilingualism refers to linguistic diversity found in a country or community.
- There is no single or simple model of multilingualism.
- Official multilingualism is a language policy adopted by a state to recognize multiple languages.
- The use of multiple languages and dialects is the global norm found in almost every country in the world, whether officially recognized or not, and can be traced back to the very beginnings of humans' language use.
- The movement of people for political, religious, social or economic reasons helps explain global multilingualism.
- Bilingualism and multilingualism have been described as *the normal and unremarkable necessity of everyday life for the majority of the world's population* (Romaine, 2012).
- Multilingualism is essential for global communication, understanding of other cultures,

and the development of global citizenship values.

- More than half of the world's population uses two or more languages (or dialects) in everyday life.
- Multilingual speakers outnumber monolingual speakers in the world's population.

Topic 7: Bi/Multilingualism is Good for Us

> *Not only does speaking more than one language keep our brains healthy as we age, but it has multiple benefits for children too, such as giving them an academic advantage and improving their employment prospects once they leave school. Moreover, multilingualism gives us access to more than one culture and improves our understanding of our own culture.*[6]

As noted above, speaking more than one language or walking in more than one language world is a bonus and an asset. It's good for the brain, good for children, useful for travel, employment and career purposes. In his popular book entitled *The Care and Education of Young Bilinguals*, Professor Colin Baker (2000),[7] a Welsh scholar of bilingualism, provides six advantages of bilingualism (Table 3). With a word of caution, Baker characterizes these advantages as *potential* because it is speakers whose two languages are reasonably balanced or fairly well-developed who enjoy the advantages listed in Table 3.

Table 3 The 6 Cs: Potential advantages of bilingualism (Baker, 2000)

Areas of Potential Advantage
Communication • greater awareness of, sensitivity to languages • ability to communicate in various contexts: family, community, worship, school, work and travel
Cultural • greater understanding of cultures • acceptance and understanding of others • access to traditions, music, stories, history, folklore and literature • understanding different ways of living
Cognitive • flexibility, sensitivity and creativity in thinking and planning • reading advantages • ability to think outside the box • understanding that the link between a word and its referent is not rigid
Character • increased self-esteem • strong sense of identity
Curriculum • doing well in school • ease in learning additional languages • transferring skills from one language into another
Cash and career • economic and employment advantages • asset in business, commerce, education and politics • wider choice of employment opportunities in the global market • careers in local, national and multinational companies

Topic 8: Bilingual Dogs[8]

If you are a dog lover, this study of canine bilingualism will make your heart sing. The brain scanning experiment summarized here shows that dogs are more than smart – they have bilingual abilities!

When Dr Laura Cuaya, a brain researcher, moved from Mexico to Hungary, she wondered how a language change would affect her dog Kun Kun: *Would he notice the change in language from Spanish to Hungarian? Would he differentiate between languages?*

To answer these two questions Dr Cuaya and her colleagues designed a unique, never-before-attempted brain scanning experiment with 18 dogs (Cuaya *et al.*, 2022). Seventeen of the dogs were Hungarian and one, Kun Kun, was Spanish. Some of the dogs were older and some were younger. All 18 dogs had heard only one language in their lives. As the dogs rested quietly in an MRI machine (shown on left) and listened to excerpts from *The Little Prince*,[9] in Spanish, in Hungarian and then in a scrambled version of both Hungarian and Spanish, Dr Cuaya and her colleagues analyzed their brain activity. Here is what they found:

- A dog brain can differentiate between languages.
- The primary auditory cortex of a dog can distinguish human speech from non-speech.
- The secondary auditory cortex of a dog can distinguish Spanish from Hungarian.

- The older the dog, the more language hearing experience, the better the understanding of speech sounds.

Topic 9: Bilingualism: Common Myths[10]

Even though research has established the value and the many cognitive benefits of using more than one language, bilingualism is still surrounded by myths, misconceptions, false beliefs, and yes, fake news. The bilingual myths presented here are adapted from the work of François Grosjean,[11] who was once described by a journalist as my *all-time favourite specialist* on bilingualism, and also from the American linguist, Mark Guiberson (2013). The 10 common myths about general bilingualism are followed by six myths about childhood bilingualism. Each myth is briefly described and is followed by a *research check* that deconstructs or debunks the falsehood.

MYTH 1: Bilingualism is a rare phenomenon

Research check   Not so! Bilingualism is a global phenomenon. More than half of the world's population uses two or more languages. Bilingualism is found in all parts of the world, at all levels of society and in all age groups.

MYTH 2: Bilinguals have equal and perfect knowledge of their two languages

Research check   This is wishful and hopeful, but untrue. In reality, bilinguals use their languages in different ways, in different contexts and with different people. Some are stronger (or dominant) in one of their languages; some are literate in both languages, while others have only passive knowledge of one of their languages. A small number of bilinguals are equally fluent in their two languages.

MYTH 3: True bilinguals have no accent in their two languages

Research check Having an accent, or *sounding different*, does not make a speaker more or less bilingual. If a second (or new) language is learned before puberty, there will be little or no trace of an accent. However, later in life, unfamiliar speech sounds of a new language become harder to master, resulting in *sounding different*. Here is an example: German adult speakers learning English encounter /w/ and /th/ at the beginning of words (wish and this). /w/ and /th/ speech sounds do not exist in German and are pronounced by adult learners as follows: *wish* > vish and *this* > zis. In the same way English speakers learning German encounter /ö/ and /ü/, two marked vowel sounds not found in English. This means that they use English vowel pronunciation when pronouncing *schön* (beautiful) and *müde* (tired).

MYTH 4: Bilinguals are born translators

Research check Bilinguals can manage simple translations from one language to another. However, translating complex topics from the stronger language into the weaker one can be difficult due to a lack of specialized vocabulary.

MYTH 5: Mixing languages is a sign of laziness in bilinguals

Research check — Language mixing, translanguaging or moving across languages is the way bilinguals *language* or talk with other bilinguals. Studies have shown that speakers of two languages, even very young bilinguals, are communicatively aware and sensitive. This means that they know when to mix their languages and with which speakers. They also know when not to mix languages. For example, a Ukrainian–English bilingual who meets a monolingual Ukrainian will use Ukrainian only.

MYTH 6: The older a person is, the harder it is to learn a second language

Research check — Age is only one factor affecting language learning. Other factors include motivation, language experience, language attitude, social context and method of language learning (formal or informal). While acquiring native-like pronunciation is easier for children, adult learners have an important advantage when learning a new language: they can transfer some skills they have developed in their native language skills, to the new language.

MYTH 7: Bilinguals are equally proficient in their two languages

Research check — Being bilingual does not mean fluency in two languages. For most bilinguals, the language they use most often becomes their dominant or stronger language. Yet, bilingualism is never fixed. Rather, it is dynamic. This means that life changes, such as age, immigration, travel, family changes, education, relationships and employment can shift a bilingual's language use, preference and dominance.

MYTH 8: Bilinguals acquire their two languages in childhood

Research check   Bilinguals acquire their languages at different times and in different contexts: from birth, in childhood, in the teenage years or in adulthood. Life situations that affect bilingualism include moving to a new country, marriage, education, employment requirements and a personal interest in languages.

MYTH 9: Bilinguals have double or split personalities

Research check   Bilinguals, like monolinguals, adapt their language to different communicative situations and people. This often leads to a change of language practice in bilinguals (e.g. a Japanese–English bilingual speaking Japanese to her grandmother and English to her sister). This change of language has led to the idea that bilinguals are different when speaking their languages. But like monolinguals, it is the situation or the person one is speaking to which creates changes in behavior, opinions or feelings, and not the fact that one is bilingual.

MYTH 10: Bilinguals express their emotions in their first language

Research check   Some bilinguals grow up learning two languages simultaneously and hence have two first languages that they use to express their emotions. For the majority of bilinguals who have acquired their languages successively, first one and then another one, the pattern is not clear. Emotions and bilingualism produce a very complicated but also very personal reality that has no set rules. Some bilinguals prefer to use one language, some the other, and some use both to express their feelings and emotions.

Topic 10: Childhood Bilingualism: Common Myths

MYTH 1: Bilingualism will delay language acquisition in children

Research check   This myth has been around for a very long time. Yet numerous research studies have shown that bilingual children are *not* delayed in their dual language acquisition. Navigating two languages does make normally developing bilingual children different than their monolingual peers, but not in the rate of language acquisition.

MYTH 2: Young children learn a second language with ease

They require no support because they simply soak up languages.

Research check   Young children are not language sponges. To learn a second or additional language they require a language-rich environment and meaningful interactions with the special people in their lives.

MYTH 3: Learning two languages is confusing to children

Research check   All normally developing children can learn and navigate more than one language. The confusion, most often, lies with the parents who are anxious and unsure about children's additional or dual language learning abilities.

MYTH 4: The one person – one language approach is best to help children become bilingual

Research check   The one person – one language strategy, where one parent speaks one language and the other parent speaks the other language, is only one of many strategies parents adopt to help children maintain two languages. Here are six other language strategies:

- using one language in the home and the other outside the home;
- assigning a language for each room in the house;
- choosing a dinner language;
- socializing with speakers of the same language;
- employing babysitters who are speakers of the same language; and
- sharing books and songs with children on a daily basis.[12]

MYTH 5: Using the home language will hinder children's progress in the school language

Research check The opposite is true. Many of the skills children develop in the home language can be transferred to the school language.

MYTH 6: Children raised bilingual will always mix their languages

Research check Bilingual children, like all bilinguals, strategically mix languages. Their sensitivity to communicative contexts and speakers guides their language choices. They use both languages with bilinguals, but not with single language speakers.

Topic 11: Translate or Interpret?

[?] The words *translate* and *interpret* are often considered similar and are used interchangeably. While this is not completely wrong, it is not completely right either. There are more differences than similarities between translation and interpretation (Crystal, 2005). Let's take a closer look.

Similarities

Translation and interpretation are two closely related linguistic disciplines. Translators and interpreters are professionals with training in linguistics and in-depth knowledge of the specific languages they work with. Their goals are the same: converting messages from one language to another. However, their work is never word-to-word conversion; rather, they focus on the *meaning* of the words they are working with.

Differences

Translators work with texts (scripts, legal, technical or medical documents) to convert information from one language into another language. They need time to do their work. Their working tools include dictionaries, thesauruses (thesauri), phrasebooks and style guides. They proofread their translations for accuracy and clarity. In contrast to translators' text-to-text task, interpreters work with spoken language in real time or on the spot: at presentations, conferences, meetings and media events. They listen to speech in one language and orally convey its meaning into another language. They also perform this in reverse between two languages to help two parties communicate.

Topic 12: Sign Language

Sign language is a visual means of communication using hand signals, gestures, facial expressions and body language. A *full language in all respects* (Roberts, 2017: 2), sign language is sometimes referred to as a language of the eye rather than the ear.[13] Based on the idea that sight is the most useful tool a deaf person has to communicate and receive information, sign language is used primarily in Deaf and Hard-of-Hearing communities. Here are the main features of sign language:

- Sign language originated in France in the mid-18th century.
- There are 300 different sign languages.

- 130 sign languages are recognized worldwide.[14]
- The most commonly used sign languages are American Sign Language (ASL), British Sign Language (BSL) and French Sign Language (FSL).
- Sign language has the same complexity as spoken language and is structurally distinct from spoken language.
- Sign language accesses the same brain structures as spoken language.
- It is used in education, commerce, government, medical and social service settings, and religious practice.
- More than 150 million people worldwide use sign language.
- More than 80% of them live in developing countries.
- The United Nations Convention on the Rights of Persons with Disabilities recognizes and promotes the use of sign languages.
- International sign language is not as complex as natural sign languages, has a limited lexicon and is used by deaf people in international meetings and informally when traveling and socializing.
- People with disabilities, including autism, apraxia of speech (speech sound disorders), cerebral palsy and Down syndrome, also use sign language.
- Baby Sign Language is used with non-verbal infants. It is a set of simple hand gestures and movements, known as signs, that correspond to first words used by young children (more, eat, milk, all gone, mom and dad).
- Baseball coaches and players use hand signs to communicate on the field.[15]

Topic 13: Forgotten and Lost Languages

Most people, who no longer use their first language, or the language they spoke in their childhood years feel a sense of loss, regret, shame, and even guilt. Many *wish* they could still speak it to reconnect with family members, communicate with locals when they visit their country of origin and regain the culture that was once important in their lives. What follows is good news for language forgetters: *relearning your first language is possible!* Let's consider three questions:

What does it mean to forget a language?

- Forgetting a language is a natural process that occurs over time.
- It is not a result of brain degeneration or age-related cognitive impairment.
- Language loss happens on an individual (not societal) level.
- It happens when a new language is learned and the speaker simultaneously navigates two languages.
- The brain inhibits the known language to make room for the increased use of a new language.
- Two language systems compete with each other.
- Language loss occurs due to decreased contact and use.
- It is most often accompanied by language shift or full move to a new language.
- First steps of language loss can be seen in the length of time needed to retrieve words.
- Language loss is found in children who speak a home language that is different from the school

language and also in adults who emigrate to a country with a different language.

- Features of language loss include lack of fluency, mixing up words, difficulty with complex grammatical structures such as clauses, pronouns and verb tenses.
- Language loss can be deeply upsetting, and can negatively affect family and social communication.

Is a forgotten language lost forever?

> *There's got to be a residue of the language somewhere. You can't really erase the system.*[16]

- A learned language is never totally forgotten.
- A speaker loses the ability to bring a forgotten language to the surface.
- Language loss need not be permanent.
- Much of a previously acquired language remains in long-term memory.
- In adults, the first language is unlikely to disappear entirely except in extreme circumstances.
- People who are *good at language learning* better preserve their first language regardless of how long they have been away from it.

Can a forgotten or a lost language be relearned or revived?

- Language revival or language relearning refers to attempts to return a language to its former use.
- This is also referred to as reactivation of a passive language.

- Length of time away from a language doesn't always matter.
- Change in language input and language environment makes a difference.
- Language recovery requires a great deal of practice and time.
- Re-learning a language is easier than learning it for the first time.

Topic 14: Language Celebrations

What is a language celebration?
Why are languages celebrated?

A language celebration is a special event organized to pay respect and tribute to language. Language festivities can be local, national or international. They can focus on one specific language, on language groups or on world languages. They are important because they raise awareness and serve as reminders that languages:

- transmit and preserve traditional knowledge;
- connect people and communities;
- represent different world views;
- are linked to speakers' origins; and
- are identity markers.

What follows is a list of language celebrations. While some are international and popular, others are country specific, topic related and little known.

Canadian language celebrations

March is *Les Rendez-vous de la Francophonie* or RVF month in Canada. A national celebration, RVP is one of the largest cultural events to celebrate *la Francophonie*. Its purpose is to promote francophone culture in communities across Canada.[17]

Table 4 American language celebrations

National Grammar Day 4 March Created in 2008 by US author Martha Brockenbrough who founded the Society for the Promotion of Good Grammar (SPOGG) https://www.nationaldaycalendar.com/national-day/national-grammar-day-march-4
National Dictionary Day 16 October Commemorates the birthday of Noah Webster, who is responsible for America's first comprehensive dictionary that includes American spellings: https://www.merriam-webster.com/activities/dictionary-day
Talk Like Shakespeare Day 23 April Founded in the USA by the Chicago Shakespeare Theatre. https://www.daysoftheyear.com/days/talk-like-shakespeare-day/

International language celebrations

International Mother Language Day: 21 February[18]

In 1999, the United Nations Educational, Scientific and Cultural Organization (UNESCO) proclaimed 21 February as International Mother Language Day (IMLD). The purpose of this day is to *promote the preservation and protection of all languages used by peoples of the world and to promote unity in diversity and international understanding, through multilingualism and multiculturalism.* The theme of the 2024 International Mother Language Day, *Multilingual education is a pillar of intergenerational learning,* serves as a reminder for educators to support, protect and promote children's home languages. Resources and ideas for celebrating IMLD can be found in Chumak-Horbatsch (2012: 130) and also on the UNESCO website: https://www.unesco.org/en/days/mother-language

International Day of Multilingualism: 27 March[19]

In 2019, two European scholars combined their perspectives of multilingualism, education and health, to establish the International Day of Multilingualism to celebrate global language richness. March 27 was selected as the celebratory date because this date is engraved on the Rosetta Stone, considered the world's oldest (197 BC) multilingual text that includes two languages (Greek and Egyptian) and three scripts (Greek, Egyptian demotic and Egyptian hieroglyphics). The purpose of the International Day of Multilingualism is to celebrate and honor our multilingual world where languages exist and co-exist and to put multilingualism into the right historical and global perspective, as the norm across continents.

European Day of Languages: 26 September[20]

In 2002 the Council of Europe proclaimed 26 September as the European Day of Languages or EDL. On this day Europeans celebrate linguistic diversity, promote awareness of Europe's linguistic heritage, encourage openness to all languages, and lifelong language learning for personal development.

International Week and Day of the Deaf: Last week of September

The International Week and Day of the Deaf are celebrated in the last week of September to commemorate the 1951 establishment of the World Federation of the Deaf. The purpose of the week-long celebration is to turn attention to deaf culture, acknowledge the achievements of deaf people and promote their rights throughout the world. Resources and ideas for celebrating the International Week and Day of Week of the Deaf can be found on the UNESCO website.[21]

International Translation Day: 30 September

In 2017 the UN's General Assembly selected the last day of September, considered the feast day of St. Jerome, the patron saint of translators, to pay tribute to the work of language professionals by, *'bringing nations together, facilitating dialogue, understanding and cooperation, contributing to development and strengthening world peace and security'*. https://www.un.org/en/observances/international-translation-day

International Decade of Indigenous Languages: 2022–2032

The United Nations General Assembly proclaimed the period between 2022 and 2032 as the International Decade of Indigenous Languages or IDIL. The aim of this ten-year period is to ensure Indigenous peoples' *right to preserve, revitalize and promote their languages.*[22] The agenda of this global initiative includes information-sharing, the promotion of resources and the creation of opportunities for exchange and dialogue among a wide network of stakeholders.

United Nations Language Days celebrate multilingualism and cultural diversity[23]

In 2010, the United Nations created *language days* for its six official languages: Arabic, Chinese, English, French, Russian and Spanish. The dates were selected for their symbolic or historic significance as shown in Table 5.

Table 5   United Nations Official Language Days

Arabic   18 December This is the date the UN General Assembly designated Arabic as the sixth official language.
Chinese   20 April This date recognizes and honors Cangji, a mythical figure who is believed to have invented Chinese characters about 5,000 years ago.
English   23 April Traditionally recognized as William Shakespeare's birthday.
French   20 March This date coincides with the International Day of Francophonie.
Russian   6 June Coincides with the birthday of the Russian poet Alexander Pushkin.
Spanish   12 October Coincides with the National Day of Spain that commemorates the anniversary of Christopher Columbus's arrival to the Americas.

Source: https://en.wikipedia.org/wiki/Official_languages_of_the_United_Nations

Topic 15: Language Resources

(a) For teachers

Chumak-Horbatsch, R. (2012) *Linguistically Appropriate Practice: A Guide for Working with Young Immigrant Children*. University of Toronto Press.

Chumak-Horbatsch, R. (2019) *Using Linguistically Appropriate Practice: A Guide for Teaching in Multilingual Classrooms*. Multilingual Matters.

Crystal, D. (2007) *How Language Works: How Babies Babble, Words Change Meaning and Languages Live or Die*. Penguin Group.

Crystal, D. (2010) *The Little Book of Language*. Yale University Press.

Roberts, I. (2017) *The Wonders of Language or How to Make Noises and Influence People*. Cambridge University Press.

(b) Websites for language discovery

Academic Kids online Encyclopaedia
https://academickids.com/encyclopedia/index.php/Language
Fifty Best Free Educational Websites for Kids (2023)
https://www.mkewithkids.com/post/10-educational-websites-that-will-actually-let-you-work-for-an-hour-or-two/

(c) Books about language for children

https://atlanticbooks.ca/stories/25-books-to-help-children-love-language/
https://shepherd.com/best-books/picture-books-about-languages
https://www.theliteracynest.com/2021/08/childrens-books-about-the-history-of-the-english-language.html
https://blog.duolingo.com/

(d) Picture books about language

Davis, W., Handicott, B. and Pak, K. (2016) *Hello Atlas*. Wide Eyed Editions.

Evans, L. (1991) *Can You Count Ten Toes?* Houghton Mifflin.

Evans, L. (2006) *Can You Greet the Whole Wide World?* Houghton Mifflin.

Feder, J. (1995) *Table Chair Bear: A Book in Many Languages.* Houghton Mifflin.

Isabella, J. (2013) *Chitchat: Celebrating the World's Languages.* Kids Can Press.

Isadora, R. (2010) *Say Hello!* G.P. Putnam Sons.

Katz, K. (2006) *Can You Say Peace?* Henry Holt and Company.

Kutschbach, D. (2014) *Art: A World of Words: First Paintings, First Words in 12 Languages.* Prestel.

Newson, L. (1996) *Language. Science Mysteries.* A & C Black.

Otohata, S. (2019) *World Languages for Kids.* Blurb, Inc.

Park, L.S. (2004) *Mung-Mung: A Foldout Book of Animal Sounds.* Charlesbridge.

Park, L.S. and Durango, J. (2005) *Yum! Yuck! A Foldout Book of People Sounds.* Charlesbridge.

Prap, L. (2004) *Animals Speak.* North-South Books.

Robinson, M. (1993) *Cock-A-Doodle-Doo! What Does It Sound Like to You?* Stewart, Tabori and Chang.

Stojic, M. (2002) *Hello World! Greetings in 42 Languages Around the Globe!* Scholastic Press.

Webb, M. (2020) *The Book of Languages.* Owlkids Books.

Zutter, H. (1993) *Who Says a Dog Goes Bow-wow?* Bantam Doubleday, Dell Picture Books.

Theme 8 Summary

This theme is a language information depot. Familiarity with the definitions, facts, realities, theories, truths, myths, explanations and celebrations will help teachers extend their understanding of how language works, help them support and guide language learning, prepare them to respond to questions about language, and help them better understand their own language circumstance.

Notes

(1)   https://www.amazon.ca/How-Language-Works-Mean ing-Languages/dp/0141015527
(2)   See Themes 3 and 7 for more information on the '*Did you know that…*?' question-probes.
(3)   Genesis 11:1–9: https://biblia.com/bible/esv/gene-sis/11/1-9; https://en.wikipedia.org/wiki/Book_of_ Genesis
(4)   https://speakt.com/language-facts/
(5)   https://www.dynamiclanguage.com/50-fascinating-lang uage-facts-you-didnt-know-infographic/
https://bestdiplomats.org/most-spoken-languages-in-europe/
(6)   https://learningportal.iiep.unesco.org/en/blog/promot ing-multilingual-approaches-in-teaching-and-learning
(7)   https://www.youtube.com/watch?v = 4DwcaoI_7SE (3:09)
(8)   https://fancycomma.com/2022/02/26/studying-your-dogs-brain-with-mri/
https://www.hepper.com/can-dogs-be-bilingual/
(9)   *The Little Prince*: https://en.wikipedia.org/wiki/ The_Little_Prince
(10) See also: Theme 3: LAP+ Stands Strong, Support Pillar 6: Bilingualism is Better.
(11) https://multilingualparenting.com/prof-francois-gros jean-on-bilingualism-language-mode-and-identity/
(12) http://www.mylanguage.ca/resources.html
(13) https://www.sil.org/sign-languages
(14) https://en.wikipedia.org/wiki/List_of_sign_languages
(15) https://en.wikipedia.org/wiki/Dummy_Hoy
(16) https://www.psychologytoday.com/ca/blog/life-bilin gual/201207/can-first-language-be-totally-forgotten
(17) https://rvf.ca/
(18) https://www.un.org/en/observances/mother-language -day
(19) https://internationaldayofmultilingualism.wordpress. com/
(20) https://edl.ecml.at/

(21) https://www.un.org/en/observances/sign-languages-day; http://wfdeaf.org/iwdeaf2021/
(22) https://en.unesco.org/idil2022-2032
(23) https://press.un.org/en/2010/obv853.doc.htm
https://www.unesco.org/en/days/world-arabic-language
https://www.un.org/zh/observances/chinese-language-day
https://www.ccjk.com/lets-celebrate-english-language-day-in-the-united-nations/
https://www.un.org/fr/observances/french-language-day/
https://www.un.org/ru/observances/russian-language-day
https://www.thereisadayforthat.com/holidays/united-nations/spanish-language-day

References

Antoniou, K. and Katsos, N. (2017) The effect of childhood multilingualism and bilectalism on implicature understanding. *Applied Psycholinguistics* 38 (4), 787–833. https://www.doi.org/10.1017/S014271641600045X

Antoniou, K., Veenstra, A., Kissine, M. and Katsos, N. (2020) How does childhood bilingualism and bi-dialectalism affect the interpretation and processing of pragmatic meanings? *Bilingualism: Language and Cognition* 23 (1), 186–203. https://www.doi.org/10.1017/S1366728918001189

Baker, C. (2000) *The Care and Education of Young Bilinguals: An Introduction for Professionals.* Multilingual Matters.

Berko Gleason, J. and Bernstein Ratner, N. (2022) *The Development of Language* (10th edn). Plural Publishing.

Crystal, D. (2007) *How Language Works: How Babies Babble, Words Change Meaning and Languages Live or Die.* Penguin Group.

Cuaya, L.V., Raúl Hernández-Pérez, R., Boros, M., Deme, A. and Andics, A. (2022) Speech naturalness detection and language representation in the dog brain. *NeuroImage* 248. https://doi.org/10.1016/j.neuroimage.2021.118811

Ferretti, F., Adornetti, I., Chiera, A., Cosentino, E. and Nicchiarelli, S. (2018) Introduction: Origin and evolution of language—an interdisciplinary perspective. *Topoi* 37 (2), 219–234. https://doi.org/10.1007/s11245-018-9560-6

Gillespie-Lynch, K. (2017) Gestural theory. In T. Shackelford and V. Weekes-Shackelford (eds) *Encyclopedia of Evolutionary Psychological Science* (pp. 3444–3448). Springer. https://doi.org/10.1007/978-3-319-16999-6_3322-1

Guiberson, M. (2013) Language confusion in bilingual children. *Perspectives on Communication Disorders and Sciences in Culturally and Linguistically Diverse Populations: Bilingual Myth-Busters Series* 20 (1), 5.

Jespersen, O. (1849) *Progress in Language with Special Reference to English.* Routledge (repr., 2013).

Müller, F.M. (1996) [1861] The theoretical stage, and the origin of language. Lecture 9 from *Lectures on the Science of Language.* Reprinted in R. Harris (ed.) *The Origin of Language* (pp. 7–41). Thoemmes Press.

Roberts, I. (2017) *The Wonders of Language or How to Make Noises and Influence People.* Cambridge University Press.

Romaine, S. (2012) The bilingual and multilingual community. In T.K. Bhatia and W.C. Ritchie (eds) *The Handbook of Bilingualism and Multilingualism* (pp. 443–465). Wiley-Blackwell. https://doi.org/10.1002/9781118332382.ch18

Schmid, M.S. (2011) *Language Attrition.* Cambridge University Press.

Ulbaek, I. (1998) The origin of language and cognition. In J.R. Hurford, M. Studdert-Kennedy and C. Knight (eds) *Approaches to the Evolution of Language* (pp. 30-43). Cambridge University Press.

Wong-Fillmore, L. and Snow, C. (2000) *What Teachers Need to Know about Language.* Center for Applied Linguistics, Office of Educational Research and Improvement, Washington, DC.

In Closing ...

My multilingual teaching journey has come to an end. What started as a discovery led to the identification of school language speakers as the missing piece in multilingual teaching. The investigation that followed focused on this overlooked group of learners, characterized their language reality, made a case for including them in the multilingual teaching agenda and included a new resource for doing just that.

Looking back

Looking back on my journey, I return to the questions that guided the missing piece investigation, revisit the goals and discuss the outcomes.

Responses to questions

The *missing piece* investigation was guided by five questions[1] about the language circumstance of school language speakers and the current state of multilingual teaching. Here are the answers to those questions:

What is the language reality of school language speakers?

School language speakers have diverse and rich language skills, experiences and interests. Some have hidden, at times neglected or forgotten, home languages, and many have an organic interest in language(s). School language speakers rarely participate in multi-language activities. They remain on the sidelines of multilingual teaching, simply because they have proficiency in the school language.

Should school language proficiency exempt learners from participating in multi-language activities?

The response to this question is a resounding NO! The exclusion of learners stands contrary to the principles of equity and inclusion as stated in a recent UNESCO document: *Inclusion in Education: All means all. Inclusion in education is about ensuring that every learner feels valued and respected, and can enjoy a clear sense of belonging.*[2]

Is there a place for school language speakers in the multilingual teaching agenda?

There is indeed! Including school language speakers in the multilingual teaching agenda gives them a sense of belonging, responds to their language interests and needs, opens up new language worlds to them and extends and enriches their language knowledge and understanding.

Has the attention to school language learners and the urgency to help, integrate and support them overshadowed the language skills and needs of school language speakers?

Yes. Supporting school language learners continues to be the focus of multilingual teaching in language-rich classrooms. This means that, in most cases, the language interests and needs of *other* learners, those who are speakers of the school language, are overlooked and disregarded.

Is current multilingual teaching fully inclusive? Is it linguistically fair?

The answer to this question is a categorical NO. Multilingual teaching that centers on language support for one group and overlooks the language interests and needs of other learners cannot be called fully inclusive or linguistically fair. If the home languages of former school language learners are discounted, if native school language speakers are not included in multi-language activities, then multilingual teaching falls short of its inclusion and fairness mandate.

Goals and outcomes

The goals of the *missing piece* investigation were achieved: two distinct groups of school language speakers were identified; their diverse and rich language realities were described; a compelling case was made to include them in the multilingual teaching program, and a new resource, especially developed to support their language skills and interests, was developed.

In conclusion, it is safe to say that the main outcome or endpoint of the missing piece investigation is an extended version of multilingual teaching as illustrated in Figure 7. With previously overlooked learners on board and a new *how to* teaching tool, this pedagogy becomes fully inclusive, where *all* learners, school language learners and school language speakers engage in meaningful language activities and are provided with language support.

Figure 7 Fully inclusive and linguistically fair multilingual teaching

Looking ahead

As I think of what lies ahead, the words of Joseph M. Marshall III (2004), a Native American author, come to mind: *The end of one journey is the beginning of the next one.*[3] These inspiring and encouraging words remind me that the investigation of school language speakers is a work in progress and that more remains to be done. My next multilingual journey, then, will continue the exploration of these learners by pursuing three initiatives: collect additional information about their language lives; extend the LAP+ language engagement strategy by developing new activities and materials; and create a new space on my website (www.mylanguage.ca) for teachers to connect and share ideas and resources for supporting and enriching the language lives of school language speakers.

Final word ...

My hope is that teachers working in language-rich classrooms turn their attention to school language speakers, collaborate with language researchers, study and observe these learners, document their language behaviors, engage in meaningful dialogue about their language needs, adopt LAP+ and promote *no learner left behind* multilingual teaching.

Notes

(1) See Introduction.
(2) All means ALL: https://unesdoc.unesco.org/ark:/48223/pf0000373878
(3) Joseph M. Marshall III is a Native American who belongs to the Rosebud Sioux, Lakota tribe. He grew up in the Horse Creek Community near White River, South Dakota, USA and was raised in a traditional Lakota household by his maternal grandparents. Marshall's first language was Lakota and he learned English as a second language. He is the author of historical non-fiction about Lakota history and culture and the founder of Sinte Gleska University, a tribal college. He works as an educational and health programs administrator for the Rosebud Sioux Tribe.

References

Marshall III, J.M. (2004) *The Journey of Crazy Horse: A Lakota History.* Penguin Books.
UNESCO Global Education Monitoring Report (2020) *Inclusion and Education: All Means All.*

Index

accent 71
activism 39–41
age of second language learning 71, 72, 73
age-appropriateness (glossary) xxi
all-in mandate 23 *see also* no-learner-left-behind
Alvaro 10, 12, 43–4
ambassador roles 51
American language celebrations 82
Antoniou, K. 65
artificial languages 61
assessing progress 19, 52
aviation language 50–1, 62

Bak, T.H. 32, 33
Baker, C. 25, 67
benefits of bilingualism 25, 33, 67–8
Berko Gleason, J. 57
Bernstein Ratner, N. 57
bi-dialectalism 65
bilingual dogs 69–70
bilingualism is better 24–5
bi/multilingualism
    benefits of bilingualism 25, 33, 67–8
    bi-dialectalism 65
    common myths 70–4
    definition 66
    glossary xxi
    as a human norm 66, 70
    language role models 36
    LAP+ encourages 16
    official multilingualism 66
    passive bilingualism 9, 10, 12, 71

strength-based orientation 24
teachers' 37
Bon Appétit activity 49
book activities 46–7
books about language 48, 86–7
bow-wow theory of language evolution 58–9
Bransford, J.D. 23
bridges 31–2
Brill, P. 39
BRS 39–40

Cagliari, P. 38
Canadian language celebrations 82
career benefits of multilingualism 68
celebrations/festivities 81–5
chief opportunity orchestrators 41–2
childhood bilingualism myths 74–6
Chomsky, N. 24
Chumak-Horbatsch, R. 3, 23, 25, 44, 49, 83
classroom glossaries 48–9
classroom language ambassador roles 51
classroom language policies 32
classrooms, language-rich xxiii, 28–34
cognitive development 33, 68
collecting language information 17
competence 16, 24 *see also* proficiency
Crystal, D. 54, 59, 66, 76
Cuaya, L. 69

cultural awareness 68
Cummins, J. 16, 23, 25, 44

data sources xiv
democratic spaces 30
descriptive feedback (DF) 19, 52
dialects 64–5
'Did you know that.? question
    probe 18–19, 44, 49, 56
ding-dong theory of language
    evolution 59
documenting progress 19
dogs, bilingual 69–70
dominant language 9, 10, 71,
    72–3
dual language texts 46
Duolingo 47–8
dynamic bilingualism 30, 56, 73

Early, M. 44
emergent bilinguals 4
emotional expression 74
engagement 16–19, 30, 43–53
English-language ambassador
    roles 51
equal fluency (unlikelihood of)
    71
equality 30 see also inclusion as
    principle
European Day of Languages 84
evaluation and follow-up of LAP
    4–5
evolution of language 57–61
exposure advantage 13

fairness xiv, 93
familiar-new principle 23
Fan, S.P. 13
fast facts about language 61
Ferretti, F. 58
festivities/celebrations 81–5
Fishman, J. 24
flags 45
Flores, N. xiv
foreign language learning 11–12

forgotten languages 24, 38,
    79–81 see also language
    revival
former school language learners
    8–9, 16, 24, 31, 93
freedom 30

García, O. xiv, 4, 23, 29, 31
gardens 29–30
gesture theory of language
    evolution 60
gestures (sign languages) 77–8
Gillespie-Lynch, K. 60
global languages 49–50
glossary xxi–xxvi
Grosjean, F. 24, 70
Guiberson, M. 70

healthy linguistic diet (HLD)
    32–3
higher-order language
    knowledge 24
home languages
    home-school language
        mismatches 9, 28–9
    importance of continued
        development of 76, 93
    as intellectual resources 16
    language loss 9–10
    language revival 24, 44–8,
        80–1
How Language Works (Crystal,
    2007) 54

identities of competence 16
inclusion as principle xiv, 19, 92,
    93–4
inclusive instructional practice
    23
Indigenous languages 84–5
information about languages,
    collecting 17
informing families 17
interest in languages 11–12, 31,
    33, 48, 52

International Day of
    Multilingualism 83–4
International Decade of
    Indigenous Languages
    84–5
international language
    celebrations 83
International Mother Language
    Day 83
International Week and Day of
    the Deaf 84
interpreting 76–7

Jespersen, O. 60–1
Jude, I. 48

Katsos, N. 65
keepers 35–6
Kleifgen, J.A. 4
Kleyn, T. 31

la-la theory of language
    evolution 60–1
language, definition of 56–7
language acquisition (children)
    74
language celebrations 81–5
language discussions 17–18,
    30, 32
language engagement strategy
    16–19, 30, 43–53
language equality 30
language freedom 30
language gardens 29–30
language identities 30
language journals/logs 19, 52
language justice 23
language loss *see also* language
    revival
    Alvaro 10, 12
    forgotten languages 79–81
    glossary xxiii
    six support pillars 24
language mixing 72, 76 *see also*
    translanguaging

language opportunity
    orchestrators 41–2
language policy (classroom) 32
language profiles
    students 45
    teachers' 37
language reality (glossary)
    xxiii
language repertoires 31
language resources 86–7
language revival 24, 44–8, 80–1
language role models 36
language shift 79
language treasure troves 29
languagekeepers 35–6
language-rich classrooms xxiii,
    28–34
LAP +
    in action 43–53
    language-rich classrooms
        26–34
    new resource 15–21
    standing strong 22–7
    teachers 35–42
Li Wei 31
Liberman, Z. 13
linguistic diversity xxii
*Linguistically Appropriate
    Practice: A Guide for
    Working with Young
    Immigrant Children* or LAP
    (Chumak-Horbatsch, 2012)
    3–4
long-term memory 24, 80

Malaguzzi, L. 38
Malone, D. 31
managing a language (glossary)
    xxiv
Manyak, P.C. 16, 24
maps 50
Marshall III, J.M. 94
mastery xxiv, 52
Matt 11–12, 13, 48–51
Mehmedbegovic, D. 32, 33

monolingualism
    glossary xxiv
    native school language
        speakers 10–13
Müller, Friedrich Max 57–8
multilingual bridges 31–2
multilingual teaching agenda
    (glossary) xxv
multilingual teaching (glossary)
    xxiv
mutual intelligibility 65
myths about bilingualism 70–4

native school language speakers
        8–9, 10–13, 31
no-learner-left-behind 15, 23, 94

one-person-one-language
        approach in bilingual
        families 75
onomatopoeia, 58–9
orchestrators 41–2
origins of language 57–61
O'Sullivan, A. 40

passive bilingualism 9, 10, 12, 71
Persad, R. 16
pooh-pooh theory of language
        evolution 60
prior language knowledge 23–4
proficiency
    advantages of bilingualism 25,
        72–3, 92
    glossary xxv
    scales 19
profile of school language
        speakers 8–14

question probes 18–19, 44, 49

research methods xiv
Roberts, I. 77
role models 36
Romaine, S. 66

Schmid, M. 24
school language *see* bi/
        multilingualism
school language (glossary) xxv
second language learning in
        children 75
selection of language activities
        18
self-evaluation 19
self-text activities 45
sign languages 77–8, 84
six support pillars 22–7
Slekar, T.D. xiii
Snow, C. 55
social justice 23
speech 56–7
split personalities (bilinguals
        don't have) 73
strength-based orientation 24
support pillars 22–7

talking about language 17–18
teachers 35–42
'teaching through a multilingual
        lens' 16
theory-practice connection 6,
        38–9
thesaurus inventus 29
Tower of Babel theory of
        language evolution 59–60
translanguaging xxvi, 25, 31, 72
translation 71, 76–7
treasure troves 29

UNESCO 83, 84, 92
United Nations Language Days
        85
United Nations language
        initiatives 84–5
*Using Linguistically Appropriate
        Practice: A Guide for
        Teaching in Multilingual
        Classrooms* (LAP2)
        (Chumak-Horbatsch,
        2019) 5

Vecchi, V. 38

Wong-Fillmore, L. 55
world language facts 61–4

yo-he-ho theory of language
    evolution 59
YouTube 50